The Literacy Profiles in Practice

Toward authentic assessment

Patrick Griffin
Patricia G. Smith
Noel Ridge

Heinemann

Heinemann
A division of Reed Elsevier Inc.
361 Hanover Street
Portsmouth, NH 03801-3912

Offices and agents throughout the world

Published simultaneously in 2001
in the United States of America by Heinemann
and in Australia by
Robert Andersen & Associates Pty Ltd
433 Wellington Street
Clifton Hill, Victoria, 3068

CIP is on file with the Library of Congress
ISBN: 0 325 00399 8

Design and page make-up by Publishing Innovations
Springhill, Victoria, Australia 3444
Printed by Openbook Publishers
205 Halifax Street, Adelaide, Australia 5000

Contents

Preface

The literacy profiles were begun in Victoria, Australia, in 1986, when the research section of the Victorian Ministry of Education began a search for a system of monitoring achievement in schools. After almost five years of research and development, the first Victorian *Literacy Profiles Handbook* appeared; then followed several years of successful monitoring of school achievement. It became clear that profiling as a system of monitoring in schools also had a positive effect on teaching and learning.

Several further projects were launched, including numeracy profiles and national profiles. The Australian government adopted the idea comprehensively and developed compulsory assessment through profiles for all schools.

The profiles are descriptive, not prescriptive. The norms illustrate what is normal development for average students. No attempt is made to impose standards. Despite the benefit of such benchmarks, years of monitoring with standardized tests have not had an impact on standards to any great extent, so teachers now are given the opportunity to define what is desirable at individual student levels.

The idea of profiling was developed in the early 1990s at international conferences and at workshops with teachers in the United States, Canada, the United Kingdom, Ireland, Vietnam, Hong Kong, China and Scandinavia. It was subsequently decided to develop a set of profiles that would serve the needs of American schools, and after two years of work in the United States gathering teacher input and data on student development it was possible to make the appropriate adjustments and to provide guiding data for American teachers. This resulted in the 1995 publication of *The American Literacy Profile Scales.*

We hope that with this new series of scales the positive effect on both teaching and learning will be continued, removing the distinction between teaching and assessment — to the benefit of both teachers and students.

Acknowledgments

A book such as this cannot emerge without the help of literally thousands of people. Teachers, students, researchers, publishers and editors have all contributed to the exercise.

The Ministry of Education in Victoria, Australia, graciously agreed to the use of some of the original scales. They have been modified, but their success made it next to impossible to produce anything different — so the format remains, as does much of the content. Over the years that the scales have been in use we have received good feedback; most focused on the use of contextual information, the gap between bands D and E and the possibility of developing scales for second-language learning.

Workshops with teachers and with administrators have all contributed to the improvement of the profiles, but the most benefit has been received from users — the teachers who have shown us real applications in the classroom and how they report to parents, to administrators and to governments. These applications have been incorporated into the book.

Unlike the first handbook, this manual is based on practice. The first books were based on the authors' intuition and experience; by and large they were correct, but there can be no better advice than that which is considered good practice by users of the scales, and these people must be thanked.

Unfortunately, the great number of teachers from several countries who lent their experience and wisdom to the project makes it impossible to identify individually all who have contributed. There are, however, many who did special work for the project, particularly when time was pressing toward publication date. Jean Schultz worked hard developing ideas and trying them out in special education classes. Anne Hammond developed a range of exercises and advice for reading classes, and Bryan O'Reilly identified the breakthrough approaches to the teaching of writing associated with the profiles. John Byrne helped the teachers in northern New York to develop databases, as did Mary Driver, Joanne Scharre, Paula Fleming, Anne McCallum, Mary Vietch and Audrey Farnsworth. Without these people, it would not be possible to give teachers the advice they need in using profiles in the classroom.

Other teachers whose help is acknowledged with gratitude are as follows:

Carmel Allen, Yvonne Allen, Mary Ange, Jan Arnott, Carolyn Bartlow, Dennis Bastian, Peggy Boschma, Val Brittain, Phil Bryan, Reta S. Burns, John Burns, Nancy Campbell, Margaret Connell, Carol Coon, Marcia Cottrell, Sandra Croft, Carol Davie, Marijean Eye, Ross Grant, Kerry Hazell, Joan Hitt, Cathy Hood, Catherine Johnson, Pat Jordan, Hilary Kent, Beverly Kirpatrick, Priscilla Lawrence, Pauline Lee, Margaret Maier, Ros McArthur, Kathy McLean, James Miller, Jan Miller, Joan Mills, Lisa Moore, Helen Nissner, Peter Nix, Sue O'Brien, David Palumbo, Mary Ann Paton, Christine Powers, Cynthia Ritlinger, David Rule, Connie Russell, Monica Rylance, Sarah Salter, Anne Smyth, Cheryl Southwick, Linda Stephens, Heather Stewart, Marie Stobaugh, Jo Sullivan, Michael Sullivan, Michelle Susat, Paul Thompson, Marie Tills, Phil Toner, Tina Torcello, Marg Treloar, Veronica Tuncay, Ann Watts, Esther Wiggins, Karen Wilson, Bonnie Witt, Fay Woods, Marg Wright.

For the photographs of classroom scenes and for teaching plans used in the book, the authors wish to thank the principals, staff and students of the following schools:

PS 244, District 18, Brooklyn, New York, New York, US

PS 208, District 18, Brooklyn, New York, New York, US

PS 346, District 19, Brooklyn, New York, New York, US

PS 124, District 2, Manhattan, New York, New York, US

PS 42, District 2, Manhattan, New York, New York, US

Rolling Terrace Elementary School, Montgomery County, Maryland, US

Clopper Mill Elementary School, Montgomery County, Maryland, US

Mount Vernon Woods School, Fairfax County, Virginia, US

Enrico Fermi School, Yonkers, New York, US

School 9, Yonkers, New York, US

Oakside School, Peekskill, New York, US

Eaglehawk Primary School, Eaglehawk, Victoria, Australia

Additional photographs were supplied by Lorna Ward and consultants from Australian and United States Services in Education (AUSSIE).

Important advice regarding balanced literacy programs in schools was obtained from Ro Griffiths, Wellington, New Zealand, and Heather Ridge, Marong, Victoria, Australia.

Section 1
Profiles and assessment

Chapter 1

What is a profile?

In simple terms, a profile is a scale depicting progress in learning. There are three profile scales of literacy, to cover reading, writing, and speaking and listening; each scale covers nine levels — labelled from A (lowest) to I (highest) — and presents, at each level and in each area, a nutshell (summary) statement and a detailed description, called a *band*.

Profiles are designed to assist teachers, schools and systems with the complex process of assessment, recording and reporting of students' developing competencies and achievements.

An essential feature of a student's profile is that it shows growth. Through its ordered sequence of bands, it makes explicit what progress in learning means. It provides a framework against which evidence of

progress of an individual can be charted and achievements of a school — or even an education system — can be monitored.

Figure 1.1 highlights the overall structure of a profile scale using the nutshell statements for writing as an example. Details of the component parts — bands, nutshells and contexts — are presented in later sections that contain the classroom guidelines and materials and show the nutshell statements linked to bands of development. The nutshell encourages teachers to work first from an overview or holistic approach, focusing on levelness, and then to use the detailed bands as an indicative list of behaviors that signal growth. In short, we work from the nutshell to the detail, and then try to build the profile.

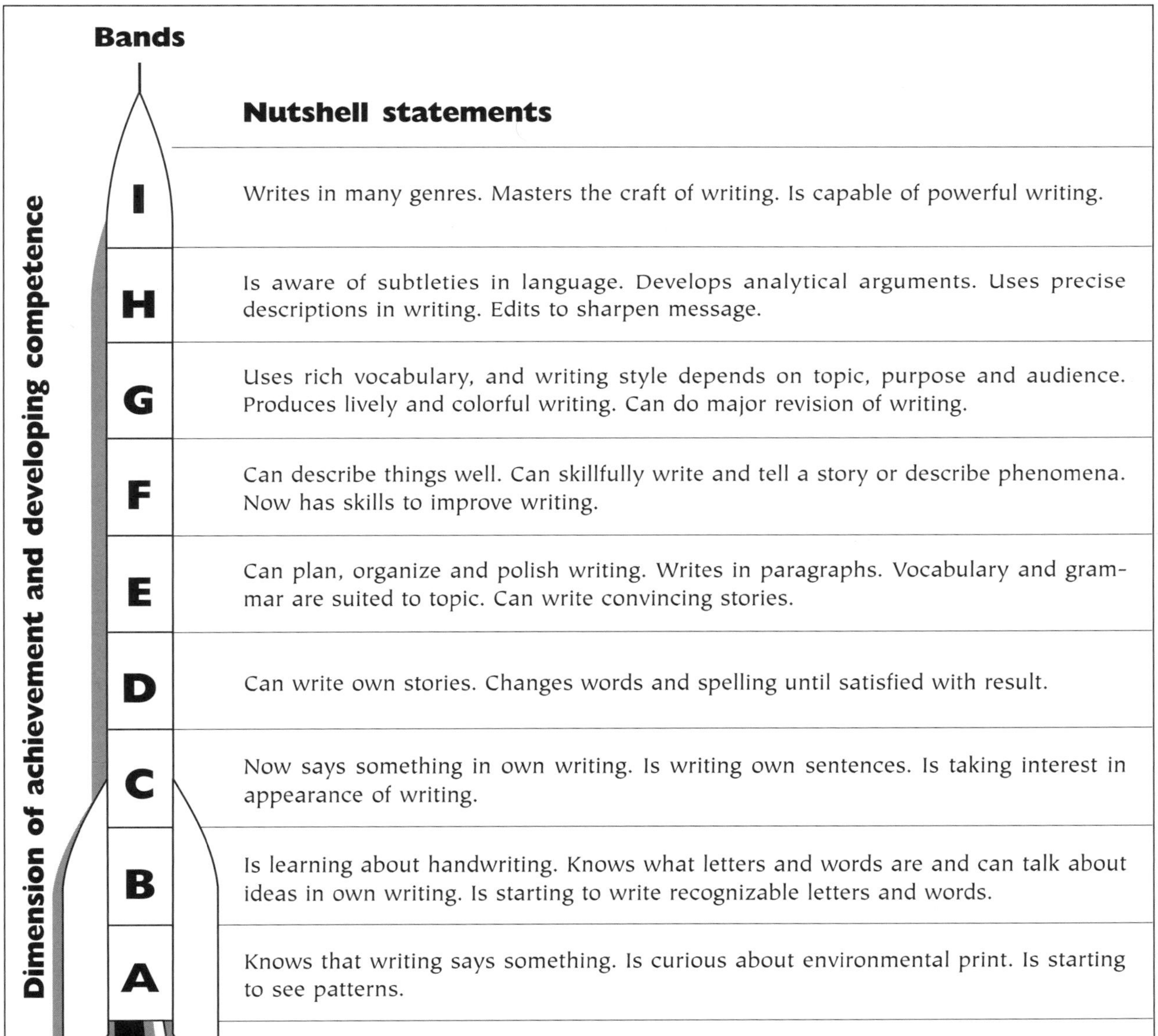

Bands

Nutshell statements

I	Writes in many genres. Masters the craft of writing. Is capable of powerful writing.
H	Is aware of subtleties in language. Develops analytical arguments. Uses precise descriptions in writing. Edits to sharpen message.
G	Uses rich vocabulary, and writing style depends on topic, purpose and audience. Produces lively and colorful writing. Can do major revision of writing.
F	Can describe things well. Can skillfully write and tell a story or describe phenomena. Now has skills to improve writing.
E	Can plan, organize and polish writing. Writes in paragraphs. Vocabulary and grammar are suited to topic. Can write convincing stories.
D	Can write own stories. Changes words and spelling until satisfied with result.
C	Now says something in own writing. Is writing own sentences. Is taking interest in appearance of writing.
B	Is learning about handwriting. Knows what letters and words are and can talk about ideas in own writing. Is starting to write recognizable letters and words.
A	Knows that writing says something. Is curious about environmental print. Is starting to see patterns.

Dimension of achievement and developing competence

Figure 1.1 Writing profile rocket

3

The relationship between the nutshell and the band is shown in the following illustration of one level (E) in each of the reading, writing, and speaking and listening bands; an example of how the profiles are presented for teachers' use is given on page 5.

Reading band E

Nutshell

Will tackle difficult texts. Writing and general knowledge reflect reading. Literary response reflects confidence in settings and character.

Band

Reading strategies

Reads to others with few inappropriate pauses. Interprets new words by reference to suffixes, prefixes and meaning of word parts. Uses directories such as a table of contents or an index, or telephone and street directories, to locate information. Uses library classification systems to find specific reading materials.

Responses

Improvises in role play, drawing on a range of text. Writing shows meaning inferred from the text. Explains a piece of literature. Expresses and supports an opinion on whether an author's point of view is valid. Discusses implied motives of characters in the text. Makes comments and expresses feelings about characters. Rewrites information from text in own words. Uses text as a model for own writing. Uses a range of books and print materials as information sources for written work. Reads aloud with appropriate expression.

Writing band E

Nutshell

Can plan, organize and polish writing. Writes in paragraphs. Uses vocabulary and grammar suited to topic. Can write convincing stories.

Band

What the writer does

Edits work to a point where others can read it; corrects common spelling errors, punctuation and grammatical errors. Develops ideas into paragraphs. Uses a dictionary, thesaurus or word-checker to extend and check vocabulary for writing. Uses vivid, specific language.

What the writing shows

Sentences with ideas that flow. Paragraphs with a cohesive structure. Ability to present relationships and to argue or persuade. Messages in expository and argumentative writing identifiable by others, although some information may be omitted. Brief passages written with clear meaning, accuracy of spelling and apt punctuation. Appropriate shifts from first to third person in writing. Consistent use of the correct tense. Appropriate vocabulary for familiar audiences such as peers, younger children or adults, with only occasional inappropriate word choice. Compound sentences, using conjunctions. Variations of letters, print styles or fonts. A print style appropriate to task and a consistent handwriting style.

Use of writing

Writes a properly sequenced text with a convincing setting. Creates characters from imagination.

Speaking and listening band E

Nutshell

Uses logic, argument and questioning to clarify ideas and understanding appropriate to audience and purpose. Accepts others' opinions and is developing listening strategies — listening for relationships in stories, poems, etc.

Band

Uses of language

Presents a point of view to a large audience. Presents materials with consideration for audience needs. Speculates and puts forward a tentative proposition. Uses logic, arguments or appeals to feelings to persuade others. Explores concepts related to concrete materials by describing, narrating or explaining how things work and why things happen. Dramatizes familiar stories, showing understanding. Uses convincing dialogue to role-play short scenes involving familiar situations or emotions. Invites others to participate. Takes initiative in raising new aspects of an issue. Asks questions to elicit more from an individual. Answers questions confidently and clearly in interviews. Asks for the meaning of familiar words used in unfamiliar ways. Listens to compare and find relationships in stories, poems, and conversations. Listens to analyze and hypothesize.

Features of language

Makes links between ideas in discussions. Uses complex connectives in speech, such as 'although', 'in spite of', 'so that'. Uses syntactical structures — principal and subordinate clauses. Uses vocabulary appropriate to audience and purpose. Distinguishes between words of similar meaning. Identifies the sounds of vowels, consonants, digraphs and blends. Uses awareness of sounds to identify consonants and vowels. Uses sounds to identify prefixes, suffixes, compounds and syllables.

Reading profile record

School .... Class ....

Name .... Term ....

Speaking and listening | Writing | **Reading**

A B C D E F G H I

	Comment
Reading band D	

Reading strategies
Reads material with a wide variety of styles and topics. Selects books to fulfill own purposes. States main idea in a passage. Substitutes words with similar meanings when reading aloud. Self-corrects, using knowledge of language structure and sound–symbol relationships. Predicts, using knowledge of language structure and/or sound/symbol to make sense of a word or a phrase.

Responses
Discusses different types of reading materials. Discusses materials read at home. Tells a variety of audiences about a book. Uses vocabulary and sentence structure from reading materials in written work as well as in conversation. Uses themes from reading in artwork. Follows written instructions.

Interests and attitudes
Recommends books to others. Reads often. Reads silently for extended periods.

	Comment
Reading band E	

Reading strategies
Reads to others with few inappropriate pauses. Interprets new words by reference to suffixes, prefixes and meaning of word parts. Uses directories such as a table of contents or an index, or telephone and street directories, to locate information. Uses library classification systems to find specific reading materials.

Responses
Improvises in role play, drawing on a range of text. Writing shows meaning inferred from the text. Explains a piece of literature. Expresses and supports an opinion on whether an author's point of view is valid. Discusses implied motives of characters in the text. Makes comments and expresses feelings about characters. Rewrites information from text in own words. Uses text as a model for own writing. Uses a range of books and print materials as information sources for written work. Reads aloud with appropriate expression.

	Comment
Reading band F	

Reading strategies
Describes links between personal experience and arguments and ideas in text. Selects relevant passages or phrases to answer questions without necessarily reading whole text. Formulates research topics and questions and finds relevant information from reading materials. Maps out plots and character developments in novels and other literary texts. Varies reading strategies according to purposes for reading and nature of text. Makes connections between texts, recognising similarities of themes and values.

Responses
Discusses author's intent for the reader. Discusses styles used by different authors. Describes settings in literature. Forms generalizations about a range of genres, including myth, short story. Offers reasons for the feelings provoked by a text. Writing and discussions acknowledge a range of interpretations of text. Offers critical opinion or analysis of reading passages in discussion. Justifies own appraisal of a text. Synthesizes and expands on information from a range of texts in written work.

Suggested new indicators

In chapters 5 to 7, the bands are collected in pages that present three levels. This has been done because in our experience with the profiles it is common for a class to be spread over three or four bands and for any individual student to exhibit behaviours described by indicators from within several adjacent bands. Hence, the profile record sheet becomes a recording procedure for teachers. The sheets are presented as blackline masters and teachers are encouraged to copy them, mark them with a highlighter pen and store them in students' portfolios.

Of the profile scales presented, those for reading and writing have been in use for some years; the speaking and listening scale is new, but has already had considerable use. Performance data has been collected for these scales.

Following chapters 1 and 2, the second section of the book first describes how to use the profiles and then presents the profile scales together with suggested authentic assessment contexts to use in the classroom.

The third section presents information on recording and reporting to a range of audiences, and shows how the scales might be used for students with special needs and discusses the reading classroom and normative data on teacher judgment.

In Appendix III, a further set of blackline masters is presented to enable teachers and administrators to make records and to adapt for reporting purposes.

Introduction to profiles

Profiles help teachers to assess and record the development of a student's literacy. The profiles are based on a belief that assessing literacy is an integral aspect of all teaching. Every aspect of a student's classroom work—worksheets, books, listening to them read, or performance tasks—can be considered as an assessment activity.

Treating assessment like this means that the distinction between teaching and assessment becomes blurred. Assessment is integrated into teaching and learning. There is really no need for an end-of-lesson test if the teacher is continuously monitoring the students' work. The records made by the teacher become the most important part of this assessment approach. Profiles help in this regard, but don't constitute all the evidence of the student's learning and development. Portfolios, reading records, reading logs, library records, running records help teachers who use a profiles approach. The profiles help in making an integrated judgment of progress.

Intervention and readiness to learn

We have recently seen a popular educational assessment method that has powerful implications for teaching. It has normally been applied to tests, but it is rarely applied in a way that helps teachers.

Developmental assessment should help teachers to monitor the student's growth. This approach asks students to do things first that they find easy, and gradually increases the difficulty of the tasks. Eventually we find that the student is no longer able to consistently display all the evidence described in the profiles. Then, as we look for evidence at even higher levels, there is less and less of the profiles that the student is able to demonstrate.

This leads us normally to conclude that we have found the student's level of achievement. But this is not strictly correct. There are three regions of development that we can identify clearly. The first is the profile level that the student has mastered or that they can demonstrate easily. The second is the set of levels of pointers that the student has difficulty with, but can show some development. The third represents those levels on the profiles that the student has not yet reached.

The second region is especially important. This is the region of intervention for the teacher. Once we know what the student is capable of doing consistently, and what the student is not yet capable of doing, we can concentrate on the region in between, and provide instruction at those levels. It is the point of intervention where the student is ready to learn.

This is an important way of thinking about developmental assessment approaches like the profiles. The level reached in a developmental continuum is not the level of achievement or the end point. It represents the point of intervention for the teacher and where the student is ready to learn. It is a starting point, not an end point.

This conclusion comes from a measurement theory that allows us to directly compare the ability of the student with the difficulty of the tasks they are asked to perform. When the student's ability is exactly equal to the difficulty of the task, the chance of success by the student is 50 per cent. It can't be considered as a level of achievement, but it is the point at which the student is most likely to develop or learn the skills and underpinning knowledge involved. Mastery and competence are found at levels where the chance of success is higher, or where tasks or behaviours are easier.

The nice thing about this way of interpreting developmental assessment is that every student has a point of intervention and the teacher can find a level at which every student is ready to learn. This way of interpreting is only applicable in a developmental assessment framework and profiles, as a developmental assessment framework, help to identify the intervention point where student is ready to learn.

In this way the profiles firmly link assessment and teaching. As teaching traces the student's development, every teaching and learning task becomes an assessment task. Each needs to be recorded in a portfolio, a log or a running record. As this is accumulated, the teacher needs to identify the point at which the student is struggling to develop, but not the point where the work is too difficult. This the point at which the learner is ready to learn or the teacher needs to intervene. It is also the point on the profiles where we can record the student's development.

This approach can therefore use a possible interpretation of test scores and apply it to profiles. However test users have almost never had the opportunity to interpret their data this way. A test score, from a properly developed test, is not an achievement score at all. If it is interpreted on a developmental continuum the score indicates the point of intervention and the student's readiness to learn. However few tests of reading are or can be interpreted this way.

So the profiles are one of the first sources of advice for teachers in this method of interpreting assessment advice. No other assessment framework currently takes this approach. The profiles therefore offer unique assistance to teachers.

Band continuums

Student . . . .

It is important to note that the reading and writing bands do not interrelate; therefore, no comparison should be made between the two.

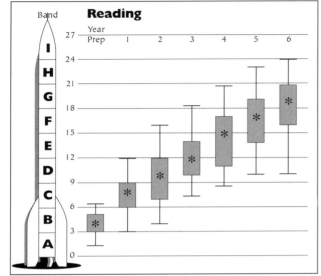

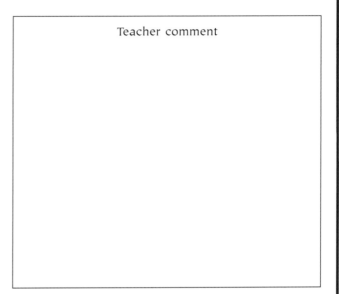

Teacher comment

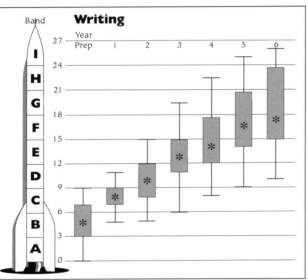

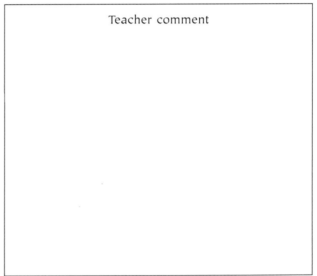

Teacher comment

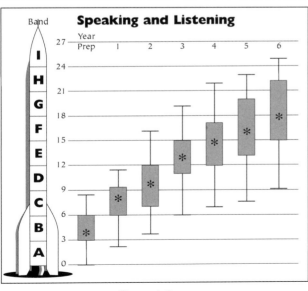

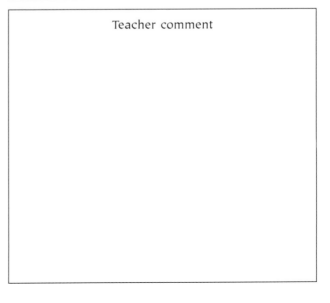

Teacher comment

Figure 1.2

Making your rocket set and class record

The box and whisker plot shows where the grade level is located on the profile scale. Select the appropriate grade level on the box and whisker plot and shade in the corresponding area on the rocket and/or the class record, depending on how you wish to report. The example shows how to do this for writing in Sixth Grade.

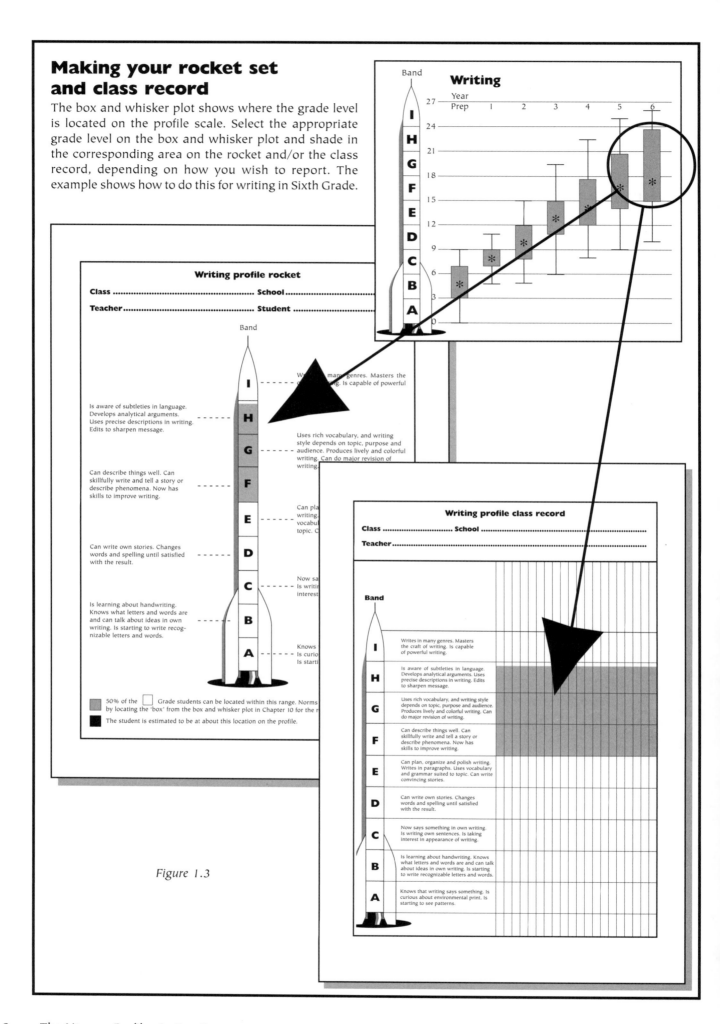

Figure 1.3

Properties of profiles

1 Profiles are holistic. Because they incorporate many kinds of learning, they allow communication of the widest span of learning outcomes: the cognitive, affective, aesthetic and practical.

2 The focus of profiles is to demonstrate competence, regardless of how it has been acquired, rather than to detail course content or be instruments of measurement. This can be across subjects and contexts, in school or at home. It does not relate to the nature of the curriculum or to the content of the texts, reading materials or the process being taught. Experience with the literacy profiles in three countries with widely varying curricula attest to their robustness in this regard.

3 The distinctive feature of profiles is that what is to be achieved is described explicitly. For example, in the scales for writing and reading an extensive range of achievement from early stages to mastery is shown regardless of how that achievement has been assessed or learnt, or of the curriculum in which the learning took place.

4 They include higher order outcomes of knowledge and skills. There is an attempt to go beyond the variations of the curriculum delivered in classrooms and to describe those things that are important for all students to know and be able to do, regardless of the details of the program that they pursue.

5 Profiles allow for a wide range of both formal methods of student assessment (tests and related assessment tasks) and informal methods (observations and descriptive judgments), typically used by teachers, to be calibrated and mapped onto a common developmental scale. Using recent developments in item response theory (IRT), the major advantage of the scales is that they make it possible for students' performances on different tasks to be compared reliably — from student to student and from year to year.

6 Profiles provide a framework for the interpretation and communication of the huge amount of assessment information available to teachers — a way of synthesizing teachers' judgments of a wide array of formal and informal assessments. They are particularly useful for interpreting performance assessment and portfolios.

7 Profiles can serve both formative and summative functions. The process of compiling profile data can be of formative use in that it may help the teaching and learning process; the product can serve summative requirements by providing overall indices of achievement for a student or group of students.

8 Profiles are often treated as qualitative, but can have quantitative components. Where there are quantitative components, data may be aggregated across subjects and/or students.

9 The interpretation of profiles is primarily criterion-referenced, but norm-referenced interpretation is sometimes also possible. Moderation, or teacher comparison of evidence and justification of judgments, is central to the application of profiling. This in turn has implications for both formal and informal professional development of teachers.

10 Finally, profiles may be motivating for students, since motivation is enhanced by emphasis on positive achievements and by allocating to the student some degree of responsibility for the compilation of the profile. Teachers may be similarly motivated by the validation profiles give their judgment and by their usefulness in identifying the positive aspects of student learning.

Chapter 2

The use and development of profiles

Uses of profiles

The process

Profiling the literacy growth of individual students has its greatest rewards for individual teachers and groups of teachers in a particular school, although the resulting profiles may also be aggregated to provide information about the larger school district. Through this manual, many uses of profiles will be mentioned, for both formative and summative assessment purposes.

Planning next lessons

When classroom teachers are planning their next lessons, topics or units of work, their knowledge of each student, based on the profiles, may enable them to target particular activities or lessons for particular students. They may group students for short periods to work on particular goals highlighted by the profile achievement patterns. Time schedules may be adjusted to meet the needs of the class based on the understandings gathered from the profiles.

Report cards

The profiles will be useful to classroom teachers as they complete reports for students. The language of the profiles is useful when making written comments for each of the students in a class.

Parent–teacher conferences

In the same way, the nutshell statements and the highlighted profile bands will become a helpful framework for conducting a parent–teacher conference, especially if the teacher has a collection of work samples from the student's portfolio, exemplifying the profile comments, to share with the parent.

Consultation between teachers

At the end of one school year, or before school starts the next Fall, profiles form an excellent basis for consultation between the 'ending' and 'receiving' teacher. Since the profile is based on objective evidence — observation and accompanying work samples — an accurate picture of the child can be passed on.

Summer school

Such information may be particularly valuable when a student has been assigned to an extended year program, in order to reach the desired grade level standard. Explicit information in a profile can be used to focus the teaching to fit the needs of the student. Since the growth in a summer school (usually 4–6 weeks) may be slight, the fact that several more behaviors on the child's profile have been highlighted may be the most valid way to describe growth over the summer.

Curriculum design

When teachers of a grade level team all use the profiles and are able to combine their observations and insights into the growth of students that the profiles provide, they may conclude that there needs to be some change in their curriculum plan, in the materials being used, or in the instructional approaches they are adopting. The profiles provide a framework for curriculum design by the teachers.

Descriptions of literacy behaviors

One of the greatest strengths of the profiles is that their descriptions of literacy behaviors are not tied to specific age or grade cohorts. Thus they may be particularly helpful in monitoring the performance of students whose growth is very atypical of their chronological age or grade placement. School organizations in the United States still require norm-referenced testing as documentation of student growth, although many changes are occurring in this regard (e.g. *The New York State Literacy Profile*). Many children do not test well, and profiles provide an alternative method of describing that child's growth.

Eliciting information from parents or caregivers

There may be times when teachers or other school staff may wish to use the framework of the profile bands to elicit information from parents or caregivers about a child's current literacy status in order to provide a starting point for teaching.

New entrants

When young children enter school for the first time they arrive with a widely varying range of literacy experiences. Many schools use an observational survey task, and the resulting information can easily be transferred to commence a student profile.

Communication with parents

Profiles provide a common language for communication between the school and home, without the problems of jargon or educational language, or difficult to communicate scores and statistical data. The profile descriptions will make it easier for parents to participate in their children's learning and to look for the next steps in their growth.

School administration

Profiles are proving of great value in focusing the attention of faculty, parents and school administrations (school or district boards) on needed changes in curriculum design and delivery. In districts where attention is focused on *English Language Arts Standards*, they are a critical tool in adjusting curriculum and teaching, so that students are able to meet new standards. Aggregated profiles are also helpful to building teams in site-based shared decision making and as a vehicle for addressing instructional reform, both at the school, and district level. (See section 3 for more detailed descriptions of such reporting procedures.)

Development of profiles

Profiles were developed to satisfy a need for more detailed descriptions of student learning. In a research project that lasted for four years, from 1986 to 1989, more than 140 teachers were involved in observing students in literacy learning situations ranging from Grade 1 to Grade 12. They were asked to monitor growth in and to document the indicators of reading, writing and spoken language behavior. The indicators of growth were then used in a series of student surveys to develop scales of growth. Thousands of students were observed and the resulting data were used to scale the indicators.

The full list of indicators was examined for patterns that might be useful in summarising the indicators into bands. Several patterns were evident in the list of calibrated indicators of reading and writing behavior. The progressions seemed to be related to underlying factors such as *attitudinal behavior, influence of reading on writing, role playing, retelling behavior, reactions to reading materials, analysis and interpretation, social or interactive roles in reading behavior, word-approach skills, types of reading materials used* and so on.

Nine bands were developed for each of reading, writing and spoken language. The number of bands, however, does not represent anything other than the apparent groupings of indicators. In fact, the original form of the reading and writing scales had seven bands, but there was a tendency to interpret the seven levels as consistent with the seven grades in a K–6 system. The project team reconstituted the teacher groups, added teachers from Grades 7–12 and then deliberately developed nine bands to avoid the correspondence with grade levels, setting band A as the earliest developmental level.

Teachers and language consultants have been consulted in several countries. The band scales were distributed to teachers and to sample groups of academics, consultants, and inspectors and other advisers in several Australian states, in the United States, New Zealand, Ireland, and the United Kingdom. They were asked to act as 'expert informants', to review the draft version of the bands and to advise on the need to edit, delete or move the indicators included in the bands or (if they considered that important indicators of the development of reading were missing) to suggest additional indicators. Advice was also sought on the structure, appropriate use and suitability of the band scales.

The profiles therefore describe indications of increasing achievement. Early levels of achievement are described in terms of beginning skills, knowledge, and concepts; the bands then progress to outline more advanced skills, deeper knowledge, and more sophisticated understandings.

The bands are meant to form a quasi-cumulative scale; that is, a student placed at band E is likely to have behavior patterns indicated by bands A, B, C and D as well as some behaviors in band E. It is not obligatory that every student exhibit all behaviors in each band. Teachers report that holistic impressions allow them to judge whether a student is beyond a band level, has not yet reached that level, or is developing the behaviors indicated at the level.

Different interpretations of development were also possible. Some teachers felt more comfortable discriminating between students who were just beginning to exhibit the behaviors in a level and those who were well into it but had not completely developed the level of competence. This interpretation of student progress was later adopted for more formal survey work during the field trials.

Data from pilot studies with the profiles provided firm support for their cumulative nature. In general, students who are rated as having established the behaviors in a particular band have already established those described in preceding bands. However, the bands are far from a stepwise sequence of development and they are not equivalent in length.

Section 2
Building profiles

Effective literacy practices in classrooms: Monitoring and assessment as part of teaching and learning

Literacy beliefs

All students come to school with individual strengths, needs and diverse literacy experiences.

By providing a teaching and learning program which focuses on building on children's existing knowledge, behaviors and attitudes, schools and teachers are best able to assist children to become successful language users.

Teaching students the strategies involved in *how to learn*, means teaching the real strategies of literacy. These strategies emphasise that language is used for learning and developing, as well as for communicating what has already been learned.

Parents are the first teachers, and are partners in the success of children.

School systems are increasingly aware of this, and actively promote close links between home and school. American Literacy Profile Scales (ALPS) is a means of connecting information from a child's out of school experiences to the classroom. The profiles have proved effective in providing a common language between home and school.

Students learn to read and write best when they have extended uninterrupted blocks of time to practice and apply skills and strategies modeled and taught by teachers and other students.

In a balanced literacy program, a minimum daily period of 90 minutes of uninterrupted time provides opportunities for teachers to model, by reading to and writing for students, working with them in small instructional groups in both reading and writing, and monitoring what they do when writing and reading for a variety of purposes, on their own. It also provides for

Immersion in meaningful print, and access to a rich array of books and other texts, fosters literacy acquisition.

a number of literacy interactions, where all language modes are used, and practiced.

Immersion in meaningful print, and access to a rich array of books and other texts, fosters literacy acquisition.
Teachers should provide a wide variety of fiction and non-fiction tests. Some are organized into levels by text difficulty, others *may* be organized by topic, author, genre and illustrator.

Students benefit from the use of a variety of flexible grouping arrangements.

A balanced mix of whole-class teaching, small-group and individual instruction, allows students to learn with, and from, each other and enables teachers to provide for personalized teaching and learning, based on information gained through careful observation. For example, the teacher may read aloud to the whole class, conduct a shared reading lesson with the whole class, or a small group, form a small group of students with similar strengths or needs for guided reading, confer individually with students, or conduct a mini-lesson with writers with similar issues that need to be addressed.

Students develop into independent, experienced readers and writers when each day includes time to be read to, to read and write with a teacher, peers and by themselves.

They are shown how to control effective reading and writing strategies, either individually or in small groups,

A typical literacy block: students learn to read and write best when they have extended uninterrupted blocks of time to practice and apply skills and strategies modeled and taught by teachers and other students.

and are given the opportunity to choose independent reading and writing challenges.

Students learn literacy best when they have real purposes for reading and writing.

In these contexts, students learn strategies that will enable them to solve problems and to use reading, writing, talking, listening and viewing as tools of learning.

Although these language modes are seen as objects worthy of study in their own right, a balanced literary program stresses language in use and provides for *learning* language, *learning about* language and *learning through* language as natural components.

The learning environment

The learning environment in a classroom, and throughout the school is an important factor. Recent research (Hill 1998, Rowe & Sykes 1996), shows the importance of establishing and maintaining a predictable, stable, routine and print-rich learning environment in each classroom.

Classrooms are filled with a wide range of reading materials from which each student can:
- select reading material — books, articles, pamphlets, short stories — to read and enjoy with confidence
- select books to explore their own interests
- select books on an independent reading level
- read books chosen by the teacher to match the student's reading needs (such as books chosen by the teacher for guided reading).

The student can continue to strengthen and build a growing control over the reading process.

The learning environment in a classroom and throughout the school is an important factor.

Classroom collections of books should include:
- libraries of high-quality books with fiction and non-fiction, poetry, short stories, magazines, and each genre represented in the Standards documents
- books for instructional purposes which are easy enough for students to read independently and practice for themselves what has been taught in the framework of literacy activities offered daily in the classroom
- multiple copies (6–8 in a set) to enable small-group guided reading teaching with a common and personalized focus

- enlarged copies of selected texts for shared reading (these texts should include commercial and class-made big books, charts, and overhead projector transparencies, and also texts that have been composed in shared writing — language experience — and interactive writing)
- portion of the classroom books which have been organized in a graded sequence (they should be graded by text difficulty, to enable students to choose books for themselves at a level at which they can be successful).

Word walls reflect children's growing knowledge of words.

Classrooms are print-rich

This print should represent and reflect the kind of daily learning and teaching activities which should occur in effective balanced literacy classrooms, and includes:
- word walls which reflect the students' growing knowledge of frequently used words, words encountered in topic studies and words resulting from sound and spelling pattern explorations
- samples of daily modeled, shared and interactive writing displayed for use as a reference for the writing workshop
- charts highlighting information which supports daily reading and writing activities (these might list the strategies used by students when they read and write successfully, or routines and schedules used in the classroom each day)
- high-quality student writing which provides exemplary models of various text types (genre) — these models may be accompanied by the standard which the sample addresses, and may also include comments pointing out why the writing meets or exceeds the appropriate standard.

The physical arrangements of the classroom

The physical arrangements should reflect the understanding that there will be whole-class, small-group and individual teaching and learning taking place each day.

These arrangements should include:
- a *meeting area*, where read aloud, shared reading, modeled and interactive writing and quality discussions can take place

Purposeful literacy activities should be planned to engage students for a sustained period of time.

- a *Big Book stand, chart easel, listening center* with tapes and copies of audio-taped books, pocket charts, an OHP where students can use it, and places where they can read and write on their own, in pairs or small groups
- *reading and writing activity centers* that are well planned and resourced at the students' level of independence so that they can use them on their own or in small groups
- *purposeful literacy activities* planned to engage students, individually or in groups, for a sustained period of time while the teacher is working with a group for guided reading, or holding an individual conference.

Some activities that teachers across grades may choose to plan are as follows.

- *Independent reading.* Students can read silently at tables, on a rug or in the class library.
- *Play reading.* A small group could read silently and then choose parts to first read out loud, and later perform.
- *Listening center.* A small group meets at the listening center with an audio tape and books chosen by the teacher.
- *Partner reading.* Students can read to and with each other, or discuss texts read silently.
- *Directed reading.* Students have non-fiction texts and clear directions for what to do with the information in them.

- *Following instructions.* Students follow written instructions exactly, to make something, or to complete a task.
- *Arranging sentence strips.* Text schema activities: reorganizing familiar texts that have been cut up.
- *Word making, alphabet and spelling activities.* Students work at tasks designed to help them understand alphabet, onset and rhyme, syllabification and other graphophonic challenges.
- *Computers with software designed to support literacy development.* These may include talking, interactive book programs, word processing and publishing programs, or intra-class networking that will enable students to chat on line or send e-mail to their classmates.

Text schema activities: arranging sentence strips to reorganize familiar texts that have been cut up.

Literacy activities in a balanced literacy classroom

In a balanced literacy classroom, the teacher plans activities in which students:

- see for themselves, through modeling and demonstration by teachers and capable peers, how reading and writing works
- join in shared reading and writing experiences, reading and writing along with the teacher and taking increasingly greater responsibility for themselves
- are guided and supported as they develop control over increasing competencies in both reading and writing

- assume full responsibility for their reading and writing, expecting to be able to overcome challenges, and solve problems on their own, or with minimum assistance
- engage in a wide variety of purposeful, planned literacy activities, designed to enable them to fully develop as highly competent readers, writers and speakers.

Explanation of literacy activities

Reading aloud to students

The practice of reading good literature to students is often referred to as *read aloud*. Ideally, the practice will occur several times a day in every classroom, for different purposes. A wide variety of materials, reflecting many genre, and a balance of fictional and factual material can be read.

Read aloud may be chosen as the approach because the text presents too many challenges for students to read on their own.

For read aloud, classrooms need:

- large quantities of quality texts providing diverse styles and levels of challenge, and prominently displayed after reading, to invite browsing
- blocks of time scheduled to ensure that the activity takes place
- teachers who demonstrate that the activity is very important for adults and children, through their own reading and sharing of texts
- teachers who model to students fluent and expressive reading, enabling some students to take responsibility for reading aloud to small groups or the whole class
- teachers who plan read aloud activities which focus on particular content areas, authors or text types, using both picture story and chapter books.

Shared reading with students

In a balanced literacy program part of the daily literacy block is designated for *shared reading*. During shared reading time, which may be 20–30 minutes each day, students gather in a specially designated place in the classroom where they sit comfortably with an unobstructed view of the big book easel, chart stand, pocket chart or overhead projector (OHP), and the teacher.

The key features of shared reading are that the teacher and the students are engaged in a daily cooperative reading experience, where all children, regardless of their ability are engaged in the reading process. They are supported by a safe environment in which the whole class is led by the teacher in the reading of a text which may otherwise be too difficult for students to read on their own. The text is best in an enlarged format, either a commercial, teacher, or class made big book, a chart or overhead projector transparency. The person leading usually uses a pointer to follow the text.

Shared reading can be used to:

- explicitly model reading strategies, including how to use meaning, structure and visual cues and how to solve problems encountered while reading
- expand students' knowledge of literature and language and their knowledge of story and text
- introduce them to new concepts and understandings from various content areas
- heighten enjoyment and understandings of poems, songs and rhymes
- demonstrate a variety of book language, print features and styles of writing
- introduce to and enable students to become familiar with the various features of the genre expected in the new, or state standards, including reports, recounts, instructional texts, fables and folk tales
- increase students' vocabulary and high-frequency word knowledge
- form a basis for planned word study and spelling investigations

Reading aloud is an important daily cooperative activity.

- help students learn about the different features in fictional and factual texts
- help them learn to use instructions, diagrams, charts, graphs and maps
- model higher order reading skills as demanded by the standards, including summarizing, identifying the main idea and supporting ideas, identifying cause and effect and discriminating between fact and opinion.

Guided reading by students

Guided reading is an approach where a teacher and a small group of students talk, read and think their way purposefully through an unfamiliar text, while working collaboratively.

The key feature of guided reading is that the teacher is using assessment information to determine individual students' strengths and needs, and forms flexible guided reading groups, based on that information.

Material for guided reading sessions is carefully selected at or around students' instructional level (90–95% accuracy rate using a running record), so that each child will be able to do most of the reading for themselves but with a little support.

For guided reading in a balanced literacy classroom, the teacher has organized the operation of the classroom so that a small group can meet uninterrupted for between 10 and 30 minutes, depending on the stage of reading and the length of the text.

There is a suitable range of texts (sets of up to 6–8 copies) to suit students' needs in guided reading. This range should include a variety of text types or genre.

Guided reading involves several steps.
- *Preparation.* In preparing for a guided reading lesson a teacher will have decided on:
  - reasons for grouping
  - material to be used
  - the major objective for the lesson
  - if and where the reading may be broken.
- *Introduction.* When introducing the text to the group,

In guided reading, the teacher guides the students to talk, read and think their way purposefully through an unfamiliar text.

the teacher ensures that the students have enough background to the text, and stimulates ideas and expectations in the group.
- *Setting purposes.* Students need to know the purpose of the guided reading. The teacher's role is to ensure they know exactly what they are reading for, how much they should read, and what to do if they finish.
- *Guiding the reading.* Students need to know the strategies they can employ to overcome obstacles during the reading. The teacher's role is to prompt and support, so that the reader is successful.
- *Discussion.* Comprehension is deepened by discussion. There should be a time to share findings, give different points of view, clarify and extend understandings by rereading, ask further questions, clear up word difficulties and perhaps develop further inquiry.

Evaluation

Questions teachers could ask themselves following a guided reading lesson may include the following.
- Did all students pursue and achieve the purposes for the reading?
- Did all contribute to lively and relevant discussion?
- How did all students' understanding deepen?
- Was there evidence of students' increasing use of appropriate strategies?
- Were students able to support points of view with confidence?
- Were they able to relate relevant experience to the reading?
- Did all meet the expected outcomes?
- Did the students enjoy the experience?

Independent reading by students

During *independent reading* time students have the opportunity to read for themselves a variety of exciting, interesting material every day.

In this block of time they are taught how to select books that they can read successfully and enjoy. To enable this, teachers organize books in predictable, accessible ways. There will be large amounts of high quality literature in the classroom libraries, grouped into appropriate levels of difficulty, representing a wide selection of interests, authors and genre.

The teacher's role will provide guidance with book choice where necessary or appropriate, including noticing when students consistently choose books beyond their control, and guiding them to make more appropriate choices.

Independent reading, scheduled into the daily literacy block, provides time for a child to practice what has been taught in whole-class, small-group and independent reading activities.

Often there will be opportunities for students to respond to what they have read, both orally and in writing. These responses may be done between reading partners or buddies.

Buddy reading can be arranged with peers, siblings, older children from other classes and adults.

During independent reading time, the teacher regularly monitors students' reading development.

Independent reading provides time for a student to practice what has been taught in class activities.

The effectiveness of independent reading will be greatly enhanced if an effective take-home book program is in operation. By reading daily to and with family members at home children may effectively double the amount of successful reading done each day and see reading as an enjoyable, rewarding and worthwhile activity.

During independent reading time the teacher routinely monitors students' reading development. Meeting with them individually, the teacher confers with them about their reading, assessing their strengths and needs, and sharing this information with them.

This useful information in the form of running records and anecdotal notes is kept as a record of the students' reading development, and is used to both inform the planning for whole-class, group and individual instruction.

Quality talk

In a balanced literacy program, daily conversations should take place with and between students in the classroom, with a particular teaching and learning focus. This may be a whole-class activity, particularly during *read aloud*, *shared reading*, *shared or interactive writing* and the sharing times that teachers plan during both reading and writing workshops. It may also be a small group activity, but should involve individual talk between teachers and students.

The teacher's role includes helping students create their own oral text, see talk written down, and use it in the classroom. Language experience, or shared writing, is a time when quality talk, resulting from a shared experience, can be written as a wall story or experience chart, which can be used later for shared reading.

In the same way interactive writing, constructed daily by the teacher and class, or the teacher and small groups, can be used later for shared reading.

Quality talk in a balanced literacy classroom may include situations where the teacher capitalizes on the experiences students have had. It involves enriched speaking and listening activities with a purpose, some of which are spontaneous, but at other times requires intentional planning by the teacher, modeling and fostering only the best conversation behaviors by students and teachers.

Quality talk involves enriched speaking and listening activities with a purpose.

Shared writing

Shared writing is an activity where the teacher and students work together to compose messages, and stories, often about a classroom activity such as a trip. The teacher's role in this is to assist composition, and scribe for the students. This approach can be used with a whole class, a group, or individual students. Shared writing demonstrates how writing works, enables students' ideas to be recorded, and creates language resources for the room.

In shared writing, teacher and students work together to compose texts.

Modeled writing

Modeled writing is generally understood as an activity where the teacher, using a chart or OHP transparency models their own thought composition and writing process, showing students how they can form intentions, write and revise, and make corrections. The difference between *modeled* and *shared* writing is the degree of active involvement by the students.

Both modeled and shared writing are ideal opportunities to demonstrate and explore how different texts, such as recount, letter, report, instructions, and narratives work.

Interactive writing

Interactive writing is an approach which can be used with students who are at the emergent and early stages of writing development. The 'shared pen' technique used in interactive writing involves them in the composition and the writing. The values of interactive writing include providing opportunities to hear sounds in the words and connect them with letters, and helping students understand 'building up' and 'breaking down' processes in both reading and writing.

Because students are sharing the pen, and actively involved in the construction and writing of the text, interactive writing provides texts that they can read independently.

Interactive writing can be used with students who are at the early stages of writing development.

Independent writing

Each day, students are provided with time and resources to do real writing for sustained periods of time, for different purposes.

During this time they use all of the strategies they have learned in other reading and writing experiences. They should see themselves as writers and authors, learning to understand the writing process.

To enable this to occur, a writing workshop time, of from 30–60 minutes daily is scheduled. In this time children are able to choose their own topics, draft, revise, correct and regularly publish their own writing.

Writing resulting from, or related to curriculum contexts areas, especially science, social studies, and mathematics can be taken through the writing process.

The teacher's role is one of support and guidance, providing 'mini lessons' which often show skills and strategies, and talking with groups or individual children during conferences which focus on meaning, clarity of message, and writing craft.

Students often share, and respond to each other's writing, providing an audience for the writer, and there are frequent opportunities for them to publish pieces, taking them through the process to produce polished, correct writing, in a variety of genre.

Guided reading and planned purposeful literacy activities

There are many ways that teachers manage a classroom to enable small groups of students to be brought together for *guided reading*.

Some teachers bring a group together while the other students are reading independently. This might be a way to start guided reading, but prevents the teacher conducting individual reading conferences and monitoring independent reading. Most teachers using a balanced literacy program adopt the following methods.

A workshop approach to literacy learning

When all students, whether in small groups, pairs, or working by themselves are engaged in purposeful literacy activities, teachers are able to bring a small group together for guided reading. Some days, teachers are able to teach 2 groups in guided reading.

The teachers are always aware that students are working at literacy activities to put into practice their ever increasing reading and writing strategies and skills.

The activities that teachers plan are based on assessment information that shows what the students can control and what they are getting under control.

This means that activity 'centres', as some call them, or 'literacy corners' or 'literacy activities' will reflect the growing understandings of the class. Activities relevant for children at the emergent stage of reading, will differ from those in a class where many of the students are reading at or beyond the fluency stage.

Teachers might consider planning and implementing some of the activities which are briefly outlined here. The teachers who planned them work in schools in Victoria (Australia), Brooklyn (New York City), Manhattan (New York City), and Yonkers (Westchester, New York).

Literacy activities for emergent and early readers

In a kindergarten or first grade class, where most students are at the emergent and early stages of reading, the following activities may be planned for.

A listening centre

Here students read along following a taped version of a book, chart, song or text. There are copies of the text for each reader. Commercial taped book sets usually have up to 3 different readings for the child to join in with. Teachers often make taped copies of poems, song and memorable class created books.

Pocket charts: cut-up story activities

The materials required are pocket charts and sentence/phrase and word strips. If you don't have pocket charts, the floor or a table is fine. Texts of books introduced in shared and guided reading, songs and poems from shared reading and texts generated in modeled and shared writing, and language experience, are reconstructed and read. The texts can be cut into sentences, phrases and often words.

Big books and enlarged texts

Here, with a small pointer, students (individuals, pairs, buddies or groups) reread familiar texts from shared reading. The texts could be those generated in modeled or shared writing or language experience. Familiar and 'well loved' texts which students return to often, provide them with the opportunity to read over and over with others.

Books for guided reading can be organised for use across grade levels.

Word walls

The word wall is a place where words encountered in reading, writing and word study are placed. Before being moved into the class or individual dictionary, words can be removed (they might be on velcro or magnets) and are used to construct sentences, and phrases from known stories, or sentences that the students compose for themselves.

Poem box

Poems that the class have read in shared reading or heard in read aloud can be collected, written on cards, and read and reread individually or in pairs or groups.

The poem box can also contain poems written by students in the writing workshop, and also poetry books. Students could take a favorite poem, copy it into their notebooks and memorize it.

Browsing boxes or book baskets

The browsing boxes or book baskets are the containers where books are placed that have become familiar, through either shared or guided reading, and students choose for themselves to read on their own or with a partner. The teacher has also placed books that they know the students in the group can read for the first time on their own.

Buddy reading

Students read together or to each other using known books from their take-home book bags.

Alphabet or ABC centre

A classroom word study centre should include many opportunities for students to work with letters and words. As an independent activity during the guided reading period, there will be specific tasks which will teach them to explore the features of letters, and to make and break words.

Literacy activities for students at and beyond the fluency stage of reading

For students who are showing more control over their reading and writing, activities that they return to each day during the reading workshop may be planned.

Research team

- Make a list of things that they want to learn more about.
- Get together with a partner who wants to find out similar things.
- Find some books from the class library that will help them find what they want to know.
- Make a bundle of information.
- Think of a way to present information to the class: a talk, a video, a hyperstack, a tape, a book or a comic.

Buddy reading

- Read a book to a friend.
- Have a book chat together.

Browsing boxes or book baskets enable students to choose their own texts for independent reading.

- Put post-it notes on pages or paragraphs that they would like to share with the class.
- Choose a phrase, sentence, or paragraph to write on a display wall.

Literature or book circles

After students have read a book or chapters of a book independently, they sign up for a literature circle. When the required number (3–5) sign up, they meet on the rug and talk about the book. Teachers help initially by modeling discussion.

Following instructions

Students are given a list of instructions that they have to follow exactly. When they have completed the task they present the finished product to the class.

Responding to texts

Activities to provide opportunities for students to deepen understanding

Readers respond to texts in a variety of ways. By encouraging students to read widely, read closely and look further into texts, teachers can help students extend their vocabularies and increase their understandings of the effects of words. They can build on understandings of the effects of words, language features and writers techniques, to help them think critically about language and meaning.

Responding to texts in a variety of ways

Teachers can provide opportunities for students to respond to texts that have been read aloud, read with them in shared reading, read by them in guided reading or independently in the following ways.

- *Directed reading.* Here the purpose is to follow instructions which relate to reading some non-fiction text. For example, before reading 'Busy as a Bee', a text which contains information about the life cycle of honeybees, the students are asked to write down 3 things that they want to know about honeybees. They then read a certain number of pages and note the information they have gained. Another task is to stop at a certain page, and write down a keyword for each event that has taken place so far in the book. They should be able to present their findings to the class.
- *Graphic organisers,* or *semantic webs.* Here the purpose is for students to read a specific text, and make a summary of the events, the plot, the characters or the setting in the story. A 'dot point' organiser would be an appropriate way of recording the details in a narrative text. Other texts have specific organisers which work best. These are *cause and effect, problem and solution* and *point of view.*
- *Setting sketches.* Students can sketch, paint or map the setting of a particular story. To do this requires close reading and investigation of the setting for the text.
- *Graphing.* Students make a graph of events or characters as they occur, rating them for importance in the story. Events can be graphed, as can their importance in the story.

Planning a literacy activity

Literacy learning activities are equally as important as the close monitoring and instruction that takes place in the guided reading lesson.

When planning small-group literacy activities, teachers need to consider the following points.

- Purposes for the activity: what will students be learning or practicing by being engaged in this activity?
- The material required: is everything that students require on hand?
- The area where the activity takes place, and directions for using the activity.
- Whether the students have clear expectations about what they are going to do. The teacher will probably have modeled this with the whole class.
- Assessment — how will they know what students have learned by taking part in the activity?

Example of a planned, purposeful literacy activity

Here is an example of an activity planned for students in a first-grade class.

Buddy reading center (for 2 pairs)

- Materials needed: small copies of the book used during shared reading. Chart of reading strategies that have been discovered amongst the students in the classroom. Independent reading book boxes.
- Purpose of the activity (expected outcomes): to practice reading, use strategies, fluent reading; develop 'reading stamina' and talk to a partner about the story.
- Procedure: pairs of students read to and with each other. They could read together, or take turns. They help and encourage each other when problems are encountered in the reading.
- Assessment: students read for expanding periods of time (they might use an egg timer, or clock to time themselves). They have discussed what they read. They are able to follow the procedure for the center. They have shared what they have read and learned at sharing time.

Establishing routines and organizing the classrooms

Classroom scheduling should provide time for a regular, planned set of literacy activities each day.

Teachers need a *minumum of 90 minutes* of uninterrupted time each day, to deliver high quality instruction, and provide effective literacy teaching for each student.

Students need opportunities to work both with assistance, on their own, and in small groups, during a typical classroom day.

Following are three typical schedules of teachers, using all the elements of a *balanced literacy program* in a designated block of time.

The first is from a classroom in New York City where the teachers, like all others in the school has an uninterrupted *block of 120 minutes*, on most days.

On days when it is not possible to get 120 minutes straight, the writing workshop takes place at another time.

Students need to have clear expectations about what they are going to do in any planned literacy activity.

Plan I

A suggested schedule for a balanced literacy class

Visible routines and managed time are essential during the daily literacy block. Each day teachers and students will follow an established routine, which could include the following:

- *Reading aloud.* Students read from a selected text, modeled or interactive writing.
- *Independent reading.* Students read books (kept in bags, baskets or magazine boxes) for themselves. These books have been introduced in guided reading, or chosen from baskets or tubs of books at their independence level. Books can be related to content area or topic study. Teachers conduct individual reading conferences, monitoring individual students' reading development. Those who are experiencing difficulty will be closely monitored and worked with on a one-to-one basis as often as practical. The aim is to understand each student's strengths and work from them.
- *Read-at-home book.* Borrowing and recording of the book is organized.
- *Shared reading.* Students gather in a designated meeting area for shared reading. The teacher has selected a big book, chart or an OHP transparency, with enlarged text to explore features of literature or language, and model and share strategies and skills that readers use to get meaning from text. A balance of fiction and non-fiction material will be used.
- *Literacy activities.* Students are allocated to small groups (centers) where planned, purposeful

independent literacy activities have been provided. They will have established routines. Expectations of work to be done, and outcomes at each center, will be clear.

- *Guided reading lesson(s).* A small group of 4–8 students are brought together for clear instructional purposes, using one copy for each student of the text that has been selected, keeping in mind their instructional level.
- *Sharing time or quality talk.* Students and the teacher come back together at the meeting area to share new learning, celebrate successes and solve problems encountered in the literacy activity time. This is a time to model and practice quality talking and listening.
- *Word study.* Students engage in clear, purposeful word solving or word study time. The focus could be on phonemic awareness (listening for sounds in words), spelling patterns (looking for patterns in words), word building or teaching strategies used in reading and writing, such as onset, rhyme and syllabification.
- *Writing workshop.* Teachers might use a structure that includes:
  - a mini-lesson, based on assessment of students' writing and observation of strategies used
  - modeled, shared or interactive writing
  - time for independent writing — at this time a small group can be drawn for assisted writing
  - individual or group conferences — to assist students in clarifying the meaning and message
  - editing, proofreading and correcting, where attention is paid to the conventions of writing
  - publishing.

- *Sharing time* (author's chair). Published pieces of writing may be shared and celebrated.

Plan 2

The following is a 90-minute *plan for a first-grade class* where classes commence at 9.00 a.m.

9.00 a.m.
Whole class

Independent reading. The teacher has provided tubs of leveled books, so the students can select their take-home books for that night. Parent volunteers work in this classroom listening to students reread the take-home books from the previous night, and help them select their new books.

The teacher usually works with up to 4 individual students, taking *running records* of their reading during this time.

9.30–10.15 a.m.
Reading workshop

Shared reading takes place with a big book, enlarged text or OHP transparency.

Small-group work

Students work in a center, organized for each activity, such as:

- the 'listen and read' center
- cut-up stories
- quiet reading, perhaps with a buddy
- working on the poetry anthology that each student is collecting
- a topic study activity related to the current class study and the guided reading group.

A balanced literacy class can include sharing time, where published pieces are celebrated and shared with the class.

Sharing circle

The students are expected on this day to use the circle time to:

- share one new aspect that they learn
- share one new skill or strategy that they will try to learn.

10.30–11.00

Writing workshop

The *writing workshop* follows a predictable routine each day, consisting of:

- *interactive writing*, which has a definite teaching focus, such as writing related sentences, hearing sounds in words and the appropriate use of capital letters
- *independent writing*
- *small groups* consisting of:
  - a teacher working with an assisted writing group
  - a group revising their drafts
  - students working on pieces for publishing
  - students proofreading and correcting each other's revised drafts
- a *sharing time* where the students are asked to listen to and read the writing of classmates, and to pay a compliment or perhaps make a suggestion about that writing.

Plan 3

A fifth-grade class

In this plan, the teacher allocates a time block of 150 minutes.

The students begin with independent reading (15–20 minutes) followed by a writing workshop (45 minutes) and interactive or shared writing (10 minutes).

The class spends 60 minutes in small-group work where the activities include two guided reading groups.

The other students in the class are engaged in buddy reading, working at the writing center, poem box, computer and reading independently.

The session concludes with shared reading and sharing time.

Using a management board

Many teachers use a *work board* to manage the classroom activity. The board includes:

- the names of students in groups — those who have the same schedule of tasks for the day are grouped together
- the names, and perhaps pictures or icons, of routine literacy tasks
- flexible ways of rotating tasks and students' names on the work board, ensuring that all experience the range of literacy events.

Conclusion

Multiple contexts for assessment are available in every classroom. They provide for many types of observations and rely on many types of validity. By following the methods of action researchers, ethnographers, anthropologists and others who study human behavior in natural settings and seek many types of data, teachers use authentic assessment. In this case the school is

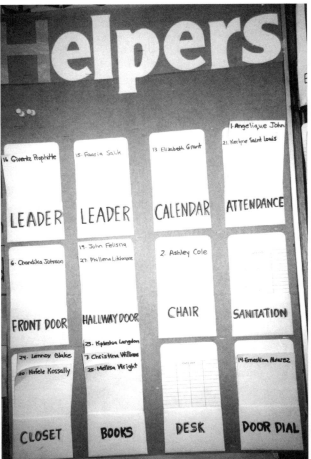

Management boards help organize classroom activities.

taken to be the natural setting for the teaching and learning process. It is possible to describe the method of triangulation as a three-stage process to observing human behavior. The first stage involves identifying the significant features, such as teaching and learning contexts and goals, the second is an intensive observation of practice and the third is a final theoretical study of principles (such as predicted performances in different settings and the psychological constructs and learning development involved.

This approach can be applied to assessment and reporting in schools. Cross-disciplinary triangulation allows similar skills demonstrated in different subject areas to be assessed. Recorder triangulation compares the views of more than one observer. Repeated observation uses the same assessment over many occasions to observe the same behavior. These triangulation methods may be used together to increase the possibility of obtaining a more consistent and more valid assessment that contains sufficient information to suit everybody's needs and purposes.

The teacher is in control of the content and context. Attitudes, interests and other affective characteristics can be assessed. These characteristics need to be given more emphasis in the assessment process in order to reflect their relative importance in the curriculum. The teacher is in control of decisions regarding what competences are valued in the school context, and so must be able to select appropriate procedures for the assessment.

Triangulation is based on a premise that no one type of measure can adequately describe any phenomenon being studied. A series of related observations, using a different referent for the performance, is likely to provide credible — or valid — information. The teacher can use the literacy profile scales, which encourage the use of multiple methods of observation and which provide criterion-referenced descriptions as part of the authentic assessment process.

Chapter 4

Getting started

Unlike a test score, which may be quick to obtain, a literacy profile takes a little time to build at first because it is complex and rich in information. This does not mean, however, that profile building has to be arduous. After a while it may become second nature to teachers and take very little time at all. It is, after all, an articulation of what teachers see and do in ordinary, everyday classrooms. Recording information about students' learning should be a simple and routine part of teaching and learning when a teacher gets into the habit of recording significant observations and judgments and when a system is provided that enables the recordings to be easily made. The literacy profiles provide such a system.

The profiles are a kind of short cut to the use of detailed anecdotal records. By presenting descriptions of typical classroom behaviors, they offer a useful observation format that requires little more than some notes or jottings about the context of the observation and any other relevant information the teacher may wish to include. Frequent but brief entries made over a whole year can build a comprehensive profile and a comprehensive component of a portfolio. The product of this operation can then be both a record of progress monitored and a report on the student.

The items listed in the bands of the profiles are not meant to be checked off one by one. The bands do not constitute a checklist; rather, they are to be read as a cluster of typical behaviors that the teacher judges to be either present or not. As experience in using them grows, teachers will gain a feeling for the typical behaviors in each of the bands.

One might, for instance, think, 'The way Christopher talks about his reading of narrative suggests band D to me. Yet his very tentative following of instructions in this technical prose is clearly band C'. Such familiarity with the bands will only come gradually, but it can be achieved; hundreds of teachers, while working on the development of the profiles, have demonstrated that it can be done without too much difficulty. Moreover, after a while teachers find the nutshell — which captures the gist of the level — more useful than the detail of the band.

Steps in building a student's literacy profile

- Choose three students in the class. They should represent widely different levels of development.
- After looking at the nutshells, observe these students closely and mark on a record page (with a highlighter pen) those indicators that each student shows on a consistent basis.
- Choose a band that best describes the typical literacy behaviors of one student.

- Scan the bands on either side of the chosen one. Remember that the range of behaviors might spread over many bands.
- Photocopy an appropriate record for reading, writing and spoken language for each of the students being profiled.
- Write the student's name on each sheet, adding the school name, class and term.
- Look particularly at the statements describing typical behaviors within a band and make a judgment as to whether they describe in general the behavior of the student. If they do, check the heading for that group of descriptors, for example, 'What the writing shows'.
- Indicate in the comment column the date at which the judgment was made.
- Jot down in the context of observation the particular task or context that provided the source of the judgment.
- Note any comments that will help in an interview with parents, in writing a report or in the direction of future learning experiences.
- Place a check against a given band (for instance band B) once all the headings have been checked.
- Record details of other assessments as they become available. These might include additional information from parents or from student self-assessment.
- For other students in the class, observe and use the nutshell statements to determine where, approximately, they are on each of the profile scales. Check estimates later by referring to the full listing of pointers in the full scales.
- Use the nutshell, then the detail.
- Decide whether for each band level, the students:
  - have not yet reached these behaviors
  - are beginning to demonstrate them
  - are developing a significant number of these behaviors
  - are beyond this band level in their growth.
  File the records in the students' portfolios.

Starting to use the profiles with only a small number of students and learning the detail with that small number makes the task of getting started much easier. Learning to focus on the nutshell statements before checking on the details in the lists also makes it easier to start profiling in the class. Before long, the content of the profiles becomes a natural extension of the teacher's language, and the detail becomes less important. The 'nutshell first' approach will help to make the profiles a natural part of the teacher's repertoire.

The teacher is not alone in profile building. Other staff members, including the librarian, have contributions to make. But there are further participants in assessment who can become committed to the collection of evidence as well: these are the students themselves and their parents. If their contribution is to be positive, they must know what to look for and how to store the information they find. Students can keep a reading log, for example, a homework log, and selected work samples as evidence of growth. Parents can record aspects of development in literacy, new interests developed and any literacy tasks worked on. Such data should ultimately be reflected on the literacy profiles record.

Profile building in practice

It is important that profile building draws on a variety of learning contexts, extends over a long period and is complemented by samples of students' work maintained in a portfolio. Judgments about students should always relate to some tangible evidence. Profile building could involve the teacher in the following way.

Daily

Writing a note or comment on the records of two or three students in each class.

Weekly

Choosing two or three students in each class and making a formal judgment about their progress through the reading and writing bands.

Each school term

Making a systematic review and update of the judgments made for each student. Perhaps, with each one, spending a few minutes going over the written work kept in the writing folder or talking about the student's comments in the reading log. Also recording relevant information gathered from parent–teacher meetings or interviews.

By the end of each term the teacher should be able to talk about every student, pointing to specific items in the relevant bands, indicating the context in which the judgments were made and illustrating the decision with materials from the portfolio.

Understanding the layout

The layout of the profile record sheets in chapters 5 to 7 has been described in chapter 1. Taking writing band E as an example, the nutshell statement is given first.

> Can plan, organize and polish writing. Writes in paragraphs. Uses vocabulary and grammar suited to the topic. Can write convincing stories.

Below this are descriptions of common classroom tasks and contexts within which teachers might make their observations — for example, modeled writing.

> *In modeled writing* the teacher, using a large chart or an OHP, shows students how they go about:
> * forming intentions
> * drafting and revising
> * proofreading and correcting, and publishing.

This is followed by the profiles record, where band E of writing behaviors is displayed together with the preceding and following bands, which are set in a smaller typeface as is shown in the example on page 5.

Note that as a result of further development following the publication of *The American Literacy Profile Scales* the Spoken language and Listening bands have been combined to form Speaking and listening, and the Viewing component has been embedded in the Reading band.

Preparation for use in the classroom

For children first entering school, the classroom teacher might photocopy the records labelled Reading band A, Writing band A and Speaking and listening band A so that they are available for all members of the class. On each one the student's name is written in the space provided. Before photocopying, the teacher can insert at the top of the sheet the name of the school and the particular class, together with the current year. Normally, these records will go to the teacher of the class in the following year. Succeeding records are added to each student's portfolio when and as required.

Teachers at other grade levels who are introducing the profiles for the first time will need to have some knowledge of their students before they can judge which is the most appropriate band to use. Some students may exhibit behaviors that spread over several bands, and thus will require two or more records.

Using the profile record sheet

Imagine a kindergarten student at about Thanksgiving. The teacher decides to start building a reading profile for that student. One heading under Reading band A is 'Interests and attitudes'; the teacher might without hesitation put a check beside this, knowing that the student 'shows preference for particular books' and 'chooses books as a free time activity'. These are typical behaviors listed under this first heading. The teacher in this case would write 'Quiet reading time' to indicate the context in which the observation used in making this judgment took place, but might well have written 'Discussion with parents' or 'Reading conference', depending on the source of the information.

When looking at another heading, 'Concepts about print', the teacher might judge that the student in question still has a long way to go. The student might indeed 'hold the book the right way up', 'turn pages from the front to the back' and 'indicate the start and end of books', but might do so very hesitantly. The teacher might use a colored highlighter pen to mark these behaviors on the record. There are many significant behaviors not yet indicated, however, and it is clear that the student is not confident enough with the basic concepts of print. There are several other typical behaviors that the teacher will look out for in the coming weeks and will perhaps mark them with a different colored pen. A color can be used to show when the indicator was achieved. The change of color indicates the rate of progress as well as what the student is achieving.

Scanning the typical behaviors listed under 'Reading strategies', the teacher might judge that insufficient evidence of the suggested behaviors are displayed by the student and not record that these behaviors are demonstrated. For 'Responses', however, he or she may confidently check the heading and perhaps note 'Shared reading' in the comments column.

By spring, the teacher might have put a check beside each of the subheadings and can confidently check the major heading Reading band A. But by this time, of course, there might be a check beside the subheading 'Responses' in Reading band B because the teacher has observed a significant number of behaviors appropriate to this level — some actually listed in Reading band B and others included by the teacher. In some cases the teacher recorded the date and the comment on the observation.

A record sheet filled out in this way serves as the basis for discussing progress with the student, the parents and other teachers, and also serves as the raw material from which the written report on literacy is prepared.

Chapter 5

Reading profile records

READING band A

Knows how a book works.
Likes to have books and stories read.
Likes to talk about stories.
Displays reading-like behavior.

Contexts for observation: Curriculum focus

The classroom
- Establish a print- and language-rich environment, presenting print in natural and meaningful contexts.
- Encourage discussion and praise critical and divergent thinking.

Reading to students
- *Read aloud* and reread favorite stories and rhymes.
- Read to students every day texts that feature rhyme, rhythm and repetition.

Reading with students
During *shared reading*:
- share big books with students, modeling reading behaviors
- use the pointer when reading enlarged texts (charts or big books) so that students can follow as you read
- show, through shared reading, conventions about print such as:
  - print is written from left to right
  - a written word is a unit of print with space either side
- talk about letters by name, relating initial letters to the sounds they represent
- relate spoken to written words in context
- draw attention to relationships between words and pictures.

Reading by students
- Provide picture books with limited text that students can 'read' to themselves and others.
- Provide opportunities for students, in pairs or on their own, to reread big books from shared reading, using a small pointer to 'copy' the teacher.
- At the listening centre, provide an audio tape of small books so students can listen and read along.
- Let students use a pointer to reread songs, charts and writing that are displayed around the room.

Assessment information
This will come from:
- *informal observations* of students during reading and writing activities
- *formal assessments* such as the *New York City ECLAS* tasks, the *Sunshine Assessment Resource Kit (Grades K-L)* (Wright Group, WA 1998), Marie Clay's *Sand and Stones* tasks, and *The Early Detection of Reading Difficulties* (Heinemann, NH 1985); these can be used to identify what individual students know about the way print is organized.

School .... Class ....

Name.. Term ....

Reading band A

Concepts about print
Holds the book right way up. Turns pages from front to back. On request, indicates the beginnings and ends of sentences. Distinguishes between upper and lower case letters. Indicates the start and end of a book.

Reading strategies
Locates words, lines, spaces, letters. Refers to letters by name. Locates own name and other familiar words in a short text. Identifies known, familiar words in other contexts.

Responses
Responds to literature (smiles, claps, listens intently). Joins in familiar stories.

Interests and attitudes
Shows preference for particular books. Chooses books as a free-time activity.

Comment

Reading band B

Reading strategies
Takes risks when reading. 'Reads' books with simple, repetitive language patterns. 'Reads', understands and explains own 'writing'. Is aware that print tells a story. Uses pictures for clues to meaning of text. Asks others for help with meaning and pronunciation of words. Consistently reads familiar words and interprets symbols within a text. Predicts words. Matches known clusters of letters to clusters in unknown words. Locates own name and other familiar words in a short text. Uses knowledge of words in the environment when 'reading' and 'writing'. Uses various strategies to follow a line of print. Copies classroom print, labels, signs, etc.

Responses
Selects own books to 'read'. Describes connections among events in texts. Writes, role-plays and/or draws in response to a story or other form of writing (e.g. poem, message). Creates ending when text is left unfinished. Recounts parts of text in writing, drama or artwork. Retells, using language expressions from reading sources. Retells with approximate sequence.

Interests and attitudes
Explores a variety of books. Begins to show an interest in specific type of literature. Plays at reading books. Talks about favorite books.

Comment

Suggested new indicators

Speaking and listening

Writing

Reading

A B C D E F G H I

READING band

Recognizes many familiar words. Attempts new words.
Will retell story from a book.
Is starting to become an active reader.
Is interested in own writing.

Speaking and listening   Writing   Reading

A B C D E F G H I

Contexts for observation: Curriculum focus

The classroom

- Establish planned, purposeful literacy activities (centers) which students use to try out their increasing reading strategies.
- Sort many books by level into baskets.
- Have students reread the guided reading book many times, to partners and adults, at school and at home.
- Start a 'take-home' book.
- Read to students every day and share your own enjoyment of reading.

Reading to students

During *read aloud*:

- read an increasing range of material
- display books that have been read and reread, inviting students to read or browse for themselves
- read several books by the one author to encourage comparison
- promote discussion that goes beyond the literal level before, during and after reading.

Reading with students

During *shared reading*:

- model reading strategies such as anticipating, predicting and reading-on
- talk about letters and words in context, pointing out distinctive features

- discuss conventions of print when reading
- show students how pictures provide clues to meaning in text
- match known chunks of letters, or words in known words, to chunks or words in unknown words
- bring students' attention to high-frequency words
- help students bring this knowledge of words in the environment when reading and writing
- help students complete sentences while following the teacher reading a big book or chart.

Reading by students

During *guided reading*:

- recognize that students may be ready for guided reading when they show they have control of directionality, one-to-one matching and a number of words they recognize on sight.

During *independent reading*:

- provide supportive text at instructional level and familiarize the students with the book.
- closely monitor reading development and actively prompt for new learning.

Assessment information

This will come from:

- anecdotal notes and running records from daily independent reading conferences
- observations made during guided and shared reading
- feedback from home via the take-home book log
- teacher–parent discussions
- retelling of what has been read, which permits the teacher to make sure judgments about the student's understanding.

Photo

School .... Class ....

Name.. Term ....

Reading band A

Concepts about print
Holds the book right way up. Turns pages from front to back. On request, indicates the beginnings and ends of sentences. Distinguishes between upper and lower case letters. Indicates the start and end of a book.

Reading strategies
Locates words, lines, spaces, letters. Refers to letters by name. Locates own name and other familiar words in a short text. Identifies known, familiar words in other contexts.

Responses
Responds to literature (smiles, claps, listens intently). Joins in familiar stories.

Interests and attitudes
Shows preference for particular books. Chooses books as a free-time activity.

Comment

Reading band B

Reading strategies
Takes risks when reading. 'Reads' books with simple, repetitive language patterns. 'Reads', understands and explains own 'writing'. Is aware that print tells a story. Uses pictures for clues to meaning of text. Asks others for help with meaning and pronunciation of words. Consistently reads familiar words and interprets symbols within a text. Predicts words. Matches known clusters of letters to clusters in unknown words. Locates own name and other familiar words in a short text. Uses knowledge of words in the environment when 'reading' and 'writing'. Uses various strategies to follow a line of print. Copies classroom print, labels, signs, etc.

Responses
Selects own books to 'read'. Describes connections among events in texts. Writes, role-plays and/or draws in response to a story or other form of writing (e.g. poem, message). Creates ending when text is left unfinished. Recounts parts of text in writing, drama or artwork. Retells, using language expressions from reading sources. Retells with approximate sequence.

Interests and attitudes
Explores a variety of books. Begins to show an interest in specific type of literature. Plays at reading books. Talks about favorite books.

Comment

Reading band C

Reading strategies
Rereads a paragraph or sentence to establish meaning. Uses context as a basis for predicting meaning of unfamiliar words. Reads aloud, showing understanding of purpose of punctuation marks. Uses picture cues to make appropriate responses for unknown words. Uses pictures to help read a text. Finds where another reader is up to in a reading passage.

Responses
Writing and artwork reflect understanding of text. Retells, discusses and expresses opinions on literature, and reads further. Recalls events and characters spontaneously from text.

Interests and attitudes
Seeks recommendations for books to read. Chooses more than one type of book. Chooses to read when given free choice. Concentrates on reading for lengthy periods.

Comment

Suggested new indicators

Speaking and listening

Writing

Reading

A B C D E F G H I

READING band C

Looks for meaning in text.
Reading and discussion of text shows enjoyment of reading.
Shares experience with others.

Contexts for observation: Curriculum focus

The classroom
- Literacy activities will reflect the students' growing understandings.
- Students are expected to choose material for their own reading from the classroom collection and also from the library.
- Increasing opportunities for retelling and responding are provided.

Reading to students
During *read aloud*:
- demonstrate understandings that all texts, narrative and informational, are written by authors who are expressing their own ideas
- draw attention to literacy devices, i.e. rhyme, repetition, alliteration
- compare and contrast stories by the same author
- invite writers to read aloud from their writing.

Reading with students
During *shared reading*:
- focus on finding high-frequency words or words with particular letter patterns in text
- focus on parts of words to aid word identification
- encourage students to reflect on own strategies for working out unfamiliar words
- continue to model how to use several sources of information as you read
- provide small copies of the shared reading big book for students to read for themselves, or with the help of an audio taped version
- use shared reading texts to investigate spelling patterns and sounds in words.

Reading by students
- In *guided reading*:
  - have students predict the content and story line using the title and illustration
  - implant new language found in the book
  - highlight key concepts
  - reinforce possible reading strategies that students need to use when reading.
- *Independent reading* should take place each day with the teacher closely monitoring reading by having students read to an adult each day.

Responding to reading
- Provide opportunities for students to express personal views about a character's actions and how they relate to their own behavior.
- Retell a story orally, in pictures or in writing. Students can draw pictures describing events in a story or poem.

Assessment information
This will come from:
- students working at planned purposeful literacy activities while *guided reading* is being taken
- *reading logs*, which can be used by students to record their opinions about literature
- *running records*, which should be taken over a period and used to record and monitor reading growth
- assessment of fluency as well as comprehension.

School .... Class ....

Name.. Term ....

Reading band B

Reading strategies
Takes risks when reading. 'Reads' books with simple, repetitive language patterns. 'Reads', understands and explains own 'writing'. Is aware that print tells a story. Uses pictures for clues to meaning of text. Asks others for help with meaning and pronunciation of words. Consistently reads familiar words and interprets symbols within a text. Predicts words. Matches known clusters of letters to clusters in unknown words. Locates own name and other familiar words in a short text. Uses knowledge of words in the environment when 'reading' and 'writing'. Uses various strategies to follow a line of print. Copies classroom print, labels, signs, etc.

Responses
Selects own books to 'read'. Describes connections among events in texts. Writes, role-plays and/or draws in response to a story or other form of writing (e.g. poem, message). Creates ending when text is left unfinished. Recounts parts of text in writing, drama or artwork. Retells, using language expressions from reading sources. Retells with approximate sequence.

Interests and attitudes
Explores a variety of books. Begins to show an interest in specific type of literature. Plays at reading books. Talks about favorite books.

Comment

Reading band C

Reading strategies
Rereads a paragraph or sentence to establish meaning. Uses context as a basis for predicting meaning of unfamiliar words. Reads aloud, showing understanding of purpose of punctuation marks. Uses picture cues to make appropriate responses for unknown words. Uses pictures to help read a text. Finds where another reader is up to in a reading passage.

Responses
Writing and artwork reflect understanding of text. Retells, discusses and expresses opinions on literature, and reads further. Recalls events and characters spontaneously from text.

Interests and attitudes
Seeks recommendations for books to read. Chooses more than one type of book. Chooses to read when given free choice. Concentrates on reading for lengthy periods.

Comment

Reading band D

Reading strategies
Reads material with a wide variety of styles and topics. Selects books to fulfill own purposes. States main idea in a passage. Substitutes words with similar meanings when reading aloud. Self-corrects, using knowledge of language structure and sound–symbol relationships. Predicts, using knowledge of language structure and/or sound/symbol to make sense of a word or a phrase.

Responses
Discusses different types of reading materials. Discusses materials read at home. Tells a variety of audiences about a book. Uses vocabulary and sentence structure from reading materials in written work as well as in conversation. Uses themes from reading in artwork. Follows written instructions.

Interests and attitudes
Recommends books to others. Reads often. Reads silently for extended periods.

Comment

Suggested new indicators

Speaking and listening   Writing   Reading

A B C D E F G H I

READING band D

Expects and anticipates sense and meaning in text.
Discussion reflects grasp of whole meanings.
Now absorbs ideas and language.

Contexts for observation: Curriculum focus

Reading to students

In *read aloud*:
- provide opportunities for students to demonstrate understanding of a text
- help students identify and talk about a diverse range of text forms including traditional and contemporary literature (both fiction and non-fiction) as well as material from magazines, newspapers and textbooks
- provide opportunities for students to respond to, analyse and use core knowledge that is accurate and relevant to interpreting texts.

Reading with students

During *shared reading*:
- use two different big books or charts to make comparisons, and contrast features of the texts or the writing styles
- identify some features, such as cause and effect, main or key issues, character traits, and subject-specific language
- analyze the plot of the story
- discuss concepts and vocabulary
- extract and organize information.

Shared reading also provides opportunities to engage in a planned *word study* investigation. Examples of planned exploration at this stage may be:
- exploring sounds and grouping according to letters representing the sound ('ay', 'ee', 'igh', etc.)
- examining high-frequency words from across the curriculum
- exploring common spelling patterns and grouping words according to their pronunciations ('th', 'sh', 'wh', 'ch', 'ph' etc.).

Reading by students

During *guided reading* many students are at the point where they are reading 'in the head' so the reading during a guided reading lesson will be silent, hence 'guided silent reading'.

Enable students to:
- confirm or reject initial predictions
- discuss initial predictions and read precisely, finding the section of the text that substantiates their predictions
- make further predictions, repeating the cycle of 'anticipate, predict, confirm or reject and read on'.

A major purpose of guided reading at this stage is for students to develop the ability to question, think and read their way deeper into the ideas in the text, and develop a wider range of strategies to solve problems encountered while they are reading.

A block of time is set aside for students to read independently. During *independent reading* students read books:

- introduced during guided reading
- selected from the 'browsing boxes', or groups of books organized by text gradient (students should be matched with books that they can read — some call this their 'just right' level)
- selected from the classroom libraries
- selected from the school library
- brought from home.

The teacher's role during this time is to conduct *individual reading conferences*. In addition to closely monitoring students' individual reading development by using *running records*, take time to:
- monitor students' book choice
- praise and encourage students when they show evidence of critical reading
- assist them to articulate their reading difficulties
- discuss with students how they solved problems
- notice their ability to *retell* what they have read
- encourage students' *responses* to what they have read.

Planned small-group literacy activities or *literacy centers* provide opportunities for students to:
- listen to and read along with tapes of both fictional and factual books, responding through journal commentary, or graphic organizers
- take part in cooperative cloze
- take part in text sequencing — where the story is cut into sections
- construct a story map
- follow directions relating to a topic study — for example, making a model as an outcome of a science experience.

Buddy reading is a valuable activity at this stage of reading development

Assessment information

This will come from:
- *running records* used to ascertain which parts of the reading process are being used efficiently, and which need work
- *reading logs*, which may simply be a list of books read, or may become a tool for students to critically review the books they read, and assess their own reading growth
- *observations during guided reading* that provide insights into the strategies that students use when reading unseen texts, and their ability to gather and deepen meaning as they read
- *portfolios of students' work*, including their reading-response journals, providing a record of growth.

School .... Class ....

Name.. Term ....

Reading profile record

	Comment
Reading band C	

Reading strategies
Rereads a paragraph or sentence to establish meaning. Uses context as a basis for predicting meaning of unfamiliar words. Reads aloud, showing understanding of purpose of punctuation marks. Uses picture cues to make appropriate responses for unknown words. Uses pictures to help read a text. Finds where another reader is up to in a reading passage.

Responses
Writing and artwork reflect understanding of text. Retells, discusses and expresses opinions on literature, and reads further. Recalls events and characters spontaneously from text.

Interests and attitudes
Seeks recommendations for books to read. Chooses more than one type of book. Chooses to read when given free choice. Concentrates on reading for lengthy periods.

	Comment
Reading band D	

Reading strategies
Reads material with a wide variety of styles and topics. Selects books to fulfill own purposes. States main idea in a passage. Substitutes words with similar meanings when reading aloud. Self-corrects, using knowledge of language structure and sound–symbol relationships. Predicts, using knowledge of language structure and/or sound/symbol to make sense of a word or a phrase.

Responses
Discusses different types of reading materials. Discusses materials read at home. Tells a variety of audiences about a book. Uses vocabulary and sentence structure from reading materials in written work as well as in conversation. Uses themes from reading in artwork. Follows written instructions.

Interests and attitudes
Recommends books to others. Reads often. Reads silently for extended periods.

	Comment
Reading band E	

Reading strategies
Reads to others with few inappropriate pauses. Interprets new words by reference to suffixes, prefixes and meaning of word parts. Uses directories such as a table of contents or an index, or telephone and street directories, to locate information. Uses library classification systems to find specific reading materials.

Responses
Improvises in role play, drawing on a range of text. Writing shows meaning inferred from the text. Explains a piece of literature. Expresses and supports an opinion on whether an author's point of view is valid. Discusses implied motives of characters in the text. Makes comments and expresses feelings about characters. Rewrites information from text in own words. Uses text as a model for own writing. Uses a range of books and print materials as information sources for written work. Reads aloud with appropriate expression.

Suggested new indicators

[Side tabs: Speaking and listening | Writing | Reading]

[Vertical tabs: A B C D E F G H I]

READING band E

Will tackle difficult texts.
Writing and general knowledge reflect reading.
Literacy response reflects confidence in settings and character.

Contexts for observation: Curriculum focus

Reading band E correlates with the level of understandings and capabilities that students need, to handle the assessment tasks that states and school districts in the USA administer at Fourth Grade (for instance, in New York State, the *English Language Assessment* (ELA) at Fourth Grade).

The approaches in the balanced literacy framework provide opportunities for teachers to focus their teaching on the key elements of the assessment tasks.

Reading to students

During *read aloud*:

*   provide opportunities to use core knowledge that is accurate and relevant by having the students use prior knowledge to respond to, analyze and interpret a number of texts read to them
*   enable students to hear and discuss a widening range of different texts which should include reports, recounts, explanations, accounts and directions
*   assist students to determine important ideas and themes in a text, and support their ideas with evidence from the text
*   read short texts to students several times while they take notes, which they can use later to write responses or reports
*   enable students to engage in quality talk by asking questions of themselves and peers, and making relevant comments and predictions during pauses in the reading.

Reading with students

Shared reading is a powerful way to show students how different texts work. In addition to commercial and teacher-made big books and charts, OHP transparencies of key details or an important section of a text can be used on an overhead projector for shared reading.

In this way important understandings such as predicting and confirming; using meaning, structure and visual cues; using picture and context cues; rereading; and reading on can be demonstrated in context.

Factual texts chosen for shared reading can be used to show students how to collect information, locate information, identify key words or phrases, relate one idea to another, and draw conclusions.

Content area texts containing information for Scientific and Mathematical understandings can be chosen for shared reading.

Reading by students

Guided reading at the fluency stage provides the necessary support to enable students to:

*   use a table of contents, glossary and index with confidence

*   integrate sources of information efficiently and use a variety of reading strategies to solve difficulties
*   demonstrate knowledge of the structure of language and of how it works
*   use evidence from text to support a point of view
*   understand the different language features that are used to persuade the reader.

Students increasingly use skills and strategies that have been modeled during shared reading, while they are reading new texts, with guidance from the teacher and support from the others in the group during guided reading.

The objectives of guided reading at this stage of development should include enabling readers to:

*   make predictions and be able to substantiate them
*   self-correct
*   reread to clarify meaning
*   read on, when encountering difficulties
*   slow down and adjust the pace of reading when reading difficult texts
*   use a variety of word-solving strategies when encountering an unknown word, including recognizing chunks or clusters of letters within words that will help them work the word out.

Students who are becoming more fluent, able readers should have longer opportunities to read independently every day.

A good variety of books including easy chapter books, and longer picture books should be provided, along with interesting non-fiction texts.

Students should be encouraged to read more and take responsibility for selecting their own books from the class, school, and community library. The teacher's role is to enable them to assess a range of materials at their 'just right' level.

As well as providing texts, the teacher will also provide information and recommendations about texts, and involve students in sharing information about particular texts that they have enjoyed or found useful.

Small-group activities or *centers* can be planned in a rotation system that students can follow easily.

Planned activities may include:

*   *reading circles*, where students reading the same title ask detailed and probing questions regarding character, plot and setting
*   *retelling*, where students are able to express their understanding — orally or in writing — about text
*   *partner reading*, where students read quietly to each other in pairs, and then question each other during discussions
*   the *listen and read center* where students gather to listen to a taped book and then follow along with

the book on the second reading. After this, students may read the book independently and make some type of response, such as a semantic web.

The listen and read center can be used to assist students to develop the skills of note taking.

During this time, plan for activities where students are involved in:
- summarizing and organizing information
- reading, and then classifying elements from the story under headings like 'old and new', 'big and little'
- reading and classifying information under headings like 'fact and opinion'
- looking for logical patterns authors have used, such as comparison and contrast, or cause and effect.

Assessment information

This will be gathered by planning a schedule so that reading conferences are held regularly with all students. They could be held during independent reading time or following a guided reading lesson.

Running records will show how the student is:
- using strategies to gather meaning
- processing information
- using different sources of information to solve unfamiliar words and show whether the level of difficulty of the text is appropriate.

Retellings and responses that students make during a *conference* give teachers a quick guide as to how well they understand the text.

Teachers should prompt or ask questions to focus the student's attention on certain points or ideas in the text.

Portfolios maintained over a student's school year or years are important measures of development.

Reading logs, kept by students to enable them to monitor progress, can be linked to some kind of literature response journal reflecting goals and accomplishments.

School .... Class ....

Name .... Term ....

Reading | **Speaking and listening** | **Writing** | **Reading** | **A B C D E F G H I**

Reading band D

Reading strategies

Reads material with a wide variety of styles and topics. Selects books to fulfill own purposes. States main idea in a passage. Substitutes words with similar meanings when reading aloud. Self-corrects, using knowledge of language structure and sound–symbol relationships. Predicts, using knowledge of language structure and/or sound/symbol to make sense of a word or a phrase.

Responses

Discusses different types of reading materials. Discusses materials read at home. Tells a variety of audiences about a book. Uses vocabulary and sentence structure from reading materials in written work as well as in conversation. Uses themes from reading in artwork. Follows written instructions.

Interests and attitudes

Recommends books to others. Reads often. Reads silently for extended periods.

Comment

Reading band E

Reading strategies

Reads to others with few inappropriate pauses. Interprets new words by reference to suffixes, prefixes and meaning of word parts. Uses directories such as a table of contents or an index, or telephone and street directories, to locate information. Uses library classification systems to find specific reading materials.

Responses

Improvises in role play, drawing on a range of text. Writing shows meaning inferred from the text. Explains a piece of literature. Expresses and supports an opinion on whether an author's point of view is valid. Discusses implied motives of characters in the text. Makes comments and expresses feelings about characters. Rewrites information from text in own words. Uses text as a model for own writing. Uses a range of books and print materials as information sources for written work. Reads aloud with appropriate expression.

Comment

Reading band F

Reading strategies

Describes links between personal experience and arguments and ideas in text. Selects relevant passages or phrases to answer questions without necessarily reading whole text. Formulates research topics and questions and finds relevant information from reading materials. Maps out plots and character developments in novels and other literary texts. Varies reading strategies according to purposes for reading and nature of text. Makes connections between texts, recognising similarities of themes and values.

Responses

Discusses author's intent for the reader. Discusses styles used by different authors. Describes settings in literature. Forms generalizations about a range of genres, including myth, short story. Offers reasons for the feelings provoked by a text. Writing and discussions acknowledge a range of interpretations of text. Offers critical opinion or analysis of reading passages in discussion. Justifies own appraisal of a text. Synthesizes and expands on information from a range of texts in written work.

Comment

Suggested new indicators

READING band

Is familiar with a range of genres.
Can interpret, analyze and explain responses to text passages.

Contexts for observation: Curriculum focus

Reading to students

During *read aloud*, plan for students to be involved in activities requiring high-level thinking demands, such as to:

- make comparisons within and among texts
- make predictions, both spontaneously and in response to teachers questions
- talk about the turning points in text
- identify and analyze the choices that authors make to convey meaning (e.g. style, voice, story openings).

Students can be expected to engage in quality talk before, during and after read aloud, when they are encouraged to:

- support their own and other students' 'thinking out loud'
- build on each other's talk naturally
- acknowledge other speakers, take turns to listen and speak, justify opinions, and respect others' points of view.

Reading aloud to students is a way of familiarizing them with the sound and peculiarities of particular genres. Draw students' attention to particular features in texts such as:

- letters — distinguishing between the language of personal and business letters
- diaries — discussing the style and type of writing used in diaries
- advertising and propaganda — noting the different language features used to persuade the reader, such as vocabulary, register, metaphor, repetition and pace.

Reading with students

Shared reading at this level of students' literacy development provides opportunities for them to learn about the strategies that are needed to read expository texts.

The strategies that students learn when reading narrative do not all automatically transfer to other kinds of texts.

Overhead transparencies, teacher-made charts, or commercial big books can be used during shared reading to model the way that readers extract and organize important information by:

- using illustrations, tables and diagrams
- showing how readers identify key information and interrelationships between ideas and transform them into graphic form.

Speaking and listening

Writing

Reading

A B C D E F G H I

Use texts related to the content area of the curriculum to develop the students' knowledge of particular text structures, such as:
- Social Studies — diaries, historical fiction, myths and legends
- Science — reports, summaries, observation notes and reports
- Math — summaries, explanations, learning logs
- Music — ballads, plays, poetry.

Shared reading, and retell, is a way of closely examining the effects of a particular text. In this procedure, students discuss possible contents of a text from reading only the title, write their predictions and share them, then read the text. After a number of readings students complete a written retelling of the passage and then compare this with the original.

Reading by students

Guided reading at this level:
- ensures that students successfully read new texts levels
- provides an opportunity for students to develop and practice the reading strategies necessary to read a wide variety of texts successfully
- gives teachers and students an opportunity to successfully explore the features of language used in a variety of texts
- enables teachers to guide students to be aware of, monitor and adjust strategies used to make meaning, and to recognise and adjust when the meaning is unclear or lost.

Some of the purposes for guided reading include:
- assisting students to be aware of:
  - background knowledge that may help in their understanding
  - purpose for reading
  - different reading styles for different purposes
  - different text organization
- monitoring the reading by:
  - checking understanding
  - summarizing, paraphrasing and synthesizing information in the text
  - integrating prior knowledge with information from new texts
  - evaluating new information to check predictions
- self-checking when reading by:
  - rereading
  - searching back and forward
  - self-questioning
  - locating the point where meaning and comprehension were confused or lost
  - adjusting the reading rate.

In addition to students reading independently for enjoyment and information, *reading circles* can be very important. They enable teachers and students and peers to jointly explore texts. Discussions can focus on style, intent, response, opinions, analysis and generalizations.

Planned literacy activities enable small groups of students to work together.

- Students who have read the same book work together to prepare a performance of part of it, with the aim of publicizing the book to others.
- Students respond to and reflect on texts by:
  - making a book jacket with inside summary
  - writing another ending to the story
  - making a big book, or picture book, of important parts of a novel
  - advertising the book in a poster.
- Students rewrite all kinds of texts for a variety of audiences:
  - developing a game that uses the plot and characters from a novel
  - making a videotaped performance of a fable or folktale
  - presenting scientific or mathematical information as a comic strip or picture story book format.
- Students take notes while carrying out mathematical procedures.
- Observations are made at a science center and information noted.

Assessment information

This can be gathered by:
- *individual reading conferences* where the teacher notes how students process print, whether the rate of reading is adjusted according to the purpose, what strategies are employed, and whether these are appropriate — the records kept of these individual conferences form the basis of anecdotal reports
- *retellings after reading*, providing information as to the student's control of:
  - meaning — recalling ideas, clarity and relevance
  - structure — organization of writing, unity between parts and whole
  - conventions — including spelling, grammar and punctuation
  - cognitive abilities — ability to predict, infer, hypothesize and generalize
- *reading logs and response*, or *learning journals* — many school districts require students to keep a book log and reading journal in which, in addition to the number and types of texts read, the quality of reading materials is recorded, reflecting students' ability to assess their own growth
- *portfolios* of material from other areas of study (Math, Science, Social Studies) demonstrating the student's ability to locate and use information from texts.

School .... Class ....
Name.. Term ....

	Comment
Reading band E	
Reading strategies	
Reads to others with few inappropriate pauses. Interprets new words by reference to suffixes, prefixes and meaning of word parts. Uses directories such as a table of contents or an index, or telephone and street directories, to locate information. Uses library classification systems to find specific reading materials.	
Responses	
Improvises in role play, drawing on a range of text. Writing shows meaning inferred from the text. Explains a piece of literature. Expresses and supports an opinion on whether an author's point of view is valid. Discusses implied motives of characters in the text. Makes comments and expresses feelings about characters. Rewrites information from text in own words. Uses text as a model for own writing. Uses a range of books and print materials as information sources for written work. Reads aloud with appropriate expression.	
Reading band F	Comment
Reading strategies	
Describes links between personal experience and arguments and ideas in text. Selects relevant passages or phrases to answer questions without necessarily reading whole text. Formulates research topics and questions and finds relevant information from reading materials. Maps out plots and character developments in novels and other literary texts. Varies reading strategies according to purposes for reading and nature of text. Makes connections between texts, recognising similarities of themes and values.	
Responses	
Discusses author's intent for the reader. Discusses styles used by different authors. Describes settings in literature. Forms generalizations about a range of genres, including myth, short story. Offers reasons for the feelings provoked by a text. Writing and discussions acknowledge a range of interpretations of text. Offers critical opinion or analysis of reading passages in discussion. Justifies own appraisal of a text. Synthesizes and expands on information from a range of texts in written work.	
Reading band G	Comment
Reading strategies	
Reads manuals and literature of varying complexity. Interprets simple maps, tables and graphs in the context of discursive text. Makes generalizations and draws conclusions from reading. Reads at different speeds, using scanning, skim-reading or careful reading as appropriate.	
Responses	
Supports argument or opinion by reference to evidence presented in sources outside text. Compares information from different sources. Identifies opposing points of view and main and supporting arguments in text. Comments on cohesiveness of text as a whole. Discusses and writes about author's bias and technique. In writing, offers critical opinion or analysis of reading materials. Distils and links ideas from complex sentences and paragraphs.	
Interests and attitudes	
Reads widely for pleasure, for interest or for learning.	

Suggested new indicators

Speaking and listening

Writing

Reading

A B C D E **F** G H I

READING
band

Reads for learning as well as pleasure.
Reads widely and draws ideas and issues together.
Is developing a critical approach to analysis
of ideas and writing.

Contexts for observation: Curriculum focus

Reading to students

During *read aloud*, assist students to use core knowledge that is accurate and relevant to the text being read, by providing the opportunity for them to:

- challenge or offer counter suggestions when others offer inaccurate or inappropriate information
- refer to charts and tables in the room, with information that has been cooperatively developed, to show conventions of different genres, and authors' purposes
- be involved in activities requiring high-order thinking, where they:
    - determine important ideas and themes in a text, and support their ideas with evidence from the text
    - ask questions of themselves, the author and the text.

Students actively use knowledge by:

- discussing, either orally or in writing, visual or sensory images from the text during and after reading, using these reflections to deepen understanding of the text
- retelling or summarizing after listening to a text.

The listening center (audio player and headphones) can be utilized for small groups. The task at the center may involve listening to a short text several times to decide on characters, plot, setting, key and supporting ideas, imagery used, sequence of events, point of view, and the kinds of words the author uses.

Understand that readers interpret texts in different ways, and that one text can have many meanings. By listening to a variety of texts, students can hear and discuss features of different genres. By listening to:

- *descriptions*, students notice details of things, events, people and situations
- *explanations*, they can notice how things work and behave, and why things behave as they do
- *instructions*, they can notice sequence of directions — order by time (first, next, later) or logic (so that, as a result, in order to).

However, the prime purpose of reading aloud — to involve students in 'a good read' — should not be forgotten.

Reading with students

Shared reading in conjunction with *modeled writing* is an ideal way to demonstrate, so students can both see and hear how to become 'expert users' of oral and written language in order to:

- control and integrate their knowledge of all four language cuing systems — meaning (semantic),

structure (syntactic), visual (graphophonic) and pragmatic, or prior knowledge

- use different ways to extract and organize information from a text
- select and use prior knowledge relevant to each text — personal experience, knowledge of the particular topic, knowledge of the text structure
- identify important knowledege in text
- select and use appropriate strategies for different purposes of reading.

When reading with students:

- model the use of column or margin notes (by using stickynote paper) to record information, mark places where meaning is confused, and help students make connections with their own experiences
- model and discuss a range of note-taking procedures and other aids to information, such as graphic organizers.

Shared reading, using enlarged texts such as poems, songs, chants, short fables and various forms of information text, is an ideal format for planned spelling, investigation or word study.

Investigations might focus on:

- sound investigations with sophisticated vocabulary focusing on homophones, such as their, they're, there; too, two, to
- selecting high-frequency words from content area texts, in addition to individual word choices
- spelling patterns, such as oe, ur, ar, ir, ough, augh, ey, ei
- common plurals, common prefixes and suffixes
- words which can be classified into word families such as run, running, ran, runs, runner, rerun, re-ran, rerunning.

Reading by students

At this stage of student development many of the texts for *guided reading* should be chosen to enable students to learn and practice the precise reading and conforming strategies necessary to extract information from information texts.

During a guided silent reading lesson, guide the group by using a mix of think (open) and know (closed) questions and prompts to:

- understand in content, the vocabulary used to describe, or inform
- talk about the genre that the writer has chosen
- analyze the elements of the genre
- use strategies for reading closely and analytically, while:
  - finding key words in the text
  - going back to confirm information
  - reading titles, subtitles, captions, headings, illustrations, photographs
- compare the information in the text with other sources
- pick up the main points in the order they occur, such as in instructions.

The *independent reading* time each day provides students with many opportunities to practice and use their developing understandings, strategies and skills.

In addition to the time (20–30 minutes) spent reading by themselves, opportunities could be created, by forming *reading circles* or *book clubs*, where students can meet from time to time to:

- articulate and analyze their own actions and responses to literature they have read
- explore plot, character, bias, validity and author's style
- make and share personal responses, comparing interpretations.

During independent reading, continue to meet individual students. The purpose of these conferences is to gather information to plan for instruction while:

- monitoring the student's reading behaviors and strategies
- monitoring the student's understanding and comprehension — of plot, characters, setting
- teaching and prompting on the spot, if developing confusions are noticed.

Literacy activities

During the time for literacy activities students may:

- read and make notes to prepare for reading circle, book club, partner reading or class discussions
- read and keep a 2-column commentary (a 'think and know' chart), where the left is for speculation and prediction, and the right is for confirmation
- keep argumentative writing notes, where they demonstrate conclusions reached while reading
- read to follow directions closely, while making a model or conducting a procedure — such as cooking from a recipe.

In providing activities such as this for individuals and small groups, the emphasis should be on enabling students to read any text, have insight into how it works and how its meaning is produced, and also have a model for their own writing.

Assessment information

This can be gathered by *individual reading conferences* — an example of questions to pose during a conference with a reader who is at this stage of reading development could be:

- how did you select the book?
- how has your reading been going?
- what have you been dong well?
- are you having any problems with your reading?
- what will you tell others about the book you are reading?
- what reading strategies have you been using?
- what do you plan to do next in reading?

Important sources of information needed to plan ongoing instruction for the student, group or class, come from:

- *running records* of the student's oral reading, on both known and unknown text
- *retellings* of the text, which will provide sources of information of, the reader's control of:
  - meaning: ideas, clarity
  - structure: organization of writing, unity between parts and whole, sequence
  - conventions: usage, punctuation and appropriate vocabulary
  - cognitive abilities: ability to infer, predict, hypothesize and generalize.

Reading profile record

School .... Class ....

Name... Term ....

Reading band F **Reading strategies** Describes links between personal experience and arguments and ideas in text. Selects relevant passages or phrases to answer questions without necessarily reading whole text. Formulates research topics and questions and finds relevant information from reading materials. Maps out plots and character developments in novels and other literary texts. Varies reading strategies according to purposes for reading and nature of text. Makes connections between texts, recognising similarities of themes and values. **Responses** Discusses author's intent for the reader. Discusses styles used by different authors. Describes settings in literature. Forms generalizations about a range of genres, including myth, short story. Offers reasons for the feelings provoked by a text. Writing and discussions acknowledge a range of interpretations of text. Offers critical opinion or analysis of reading passages in discussion. Justifies own appraisal of a text. Synthesizes and expands on information from a range of texts in written work.	**Comment**
Reading band G **Reading strategies** Reads manuals and literature of varying complexity. Interprets simple maps, tables and graphs in the context of discursive text. Makes generalizations and draws conclusions from reading. Reads at different speeds, using scanning, skim-reading or careful reading as appropriate. **Responses** Supports argument or opinion by reference to evidence presented in sources outside text. Compares information from different sources. Identifies opposing points of view and main and supporting arguments in text. Comments on cohesiveness of text as a whole. Discusses and writes about author's bias and technique. In writing, offers critical opinion or analysis of reading materials. Distils and links ideas from complex sentences and paragraphs. **Interests and attitudes** Reads widely for pleasure, for interest or for learning.	**Comment**
Reading band H **Reading strategies** Compiles own list of needed references, using bibliographies and literature-search techniques. Interprets material at different levels of meaning. Forms generalizations about a range of genres, including myth, short story. Lists a wide variety of sources read for specific learning tasks. **Responses** Identifies plot and subplot. Identifies allegory. Formulates hypothetical questions about a subject, based on prior reading. Compares and offers critical analysis of materials presented in the media. Extracts ideas embedded in complex passages of text. Displays critical opinion and analysis in written reports of reading. Identifies different authors' points of view on a topic. Reformulates a task in the light of available reading resources. Questions and reflects on issues encountered in texts. Shows understanding by being able to adopt an alternative point of view to the author's. Discusses styles used by different authors.	**Comment**

Suggested new indicators

READING band H

Is clear about own purpose for reading.
Reads beyond literal text, and seeks deeper meaning.
Can relate social implications to text.

Contexts for observation: Curriculum focus

Students who have developed the reading skills and strategies and exhibit the reading behaviors described in Reading band H are generally beyond the elementary school.

For example, in the New York City schools (*Promotion Standards, Language Arts*, Reading N.Y.C. B.Ed, 1999), the expectation for students as readers is that by the end of the Grade 7 they should:

- read and understand at least 25 books, at least four about the one subject, or by the same writer, or in one genre of literature
- show evidence of understanding their reading, in both writing and classroom discussion
- skim texts to get an overview of content or locate specific information
- evaluate how accurately and effectively an author communicates information, opinions and ideas
- compare and contrast several books, forming questions to guide further reading
- read a series of steps to accomplish a task (for example in Science, Math or Social Studies)
- use computer software to enrich reading through Internet web sites.

So the approaches of a balanced literacy framework may be used in a flexible way in classrooms where the primary focus may be content such as Science, Mathematics or Social Studies.

Reading to students

During *read aloud*, initiate questions and model inquiry. This is often called 'think aloud'.

The conversation that occurs before, during and after reading aloud can broaden knowledge and foster questioning.

The ability to read and understand non-fiction is a necessary skill for students as they pursue inquiry and research.

When reading *non-fiction* on a wide range of topics from magazines, books, newspapers:

- point out non-fiction features
- build background knowledge
- appreciate style and diction
- discuss content
- refer to charts and tables that reflect information about conventions of different genres
- make critical judgments related to the text.

Teachers often introduce a unit or topic study with read-alouds, chosen for use of vocabulary and concepts students will be learning about.

Speaking and listening

Writing

Reading

A B C D E F G **H** I

Reading with students

For older students, the *shared reading* approach provides support to make more difficult texts accessible to all students in a group or class.

The teacher takes the lead in reading, with the students following in an active way.

Shared reading can assist students developing flexible reading styles, where they use a variety of reading strategies, and can read across a variety of texts and genres for different purposes.

During shared reading:
- model the skills and strategies that are important to students — thinking critically about language and layout, discussing the author's intent, contrasting and comparing author and illustrator styles
- highlight and discuss literacy elements such as tone, theme, narration, crossing genres, suspense, flashback and foreshadowing (imagery).

Shared reading also presents opportunities where teacher and students can closely examine a text to enable them to:
- select relevant passages or phrases to answer questions without necessarily reading all the text
- formulate research topics and questions, and find relevant information from text, often linking the shared reading to modeled writing where organizers such as Venn diagrams, KWL charts and 'think and know' journals are modeled
- map out plots and character developments in literacy texts
- vary reading strategies according to purposes for reading
- make connections within texts, recognizing similarities of themes and values.

Reading by students

Because of the complexity of information texts, *guided reading* is an approach which should continue to be used to enable students to develop a wide range of reading skills and strategies across a widening range of genres.

The skills and reading behaviors include:
- skimming and scanning text (to make notes and summarize)
- maintaining meaning over longer and more complex texts
- using detailed tables of contents, indexes, and glossaries, with increasing confidence
- dealing with information presented in ways other than narrative
- adjusting reading pace to accommodate purpose, style and difficulty of material
- handling complex sentences, unfamiliar vocabulary and complex layout.

In intermediate and middle schools, because of the way that schedules are constructed, it may be difficult to block out significant time for students to do their own *independent reading*.

However, it is clear that for students to meet standards, time has to be built into school schedules to provide them with time to practice reading.

It is essential for all students to:
- be provided with time to read
- discuss their reactions to books with other readers
- have access to a wide range of literature on, above and below their independent reading levels
- choose from a wide range of books they can read independently
- be supported by the teacher, who may read aloud excerpts from selected texts
- see teachers modeling independent reading by reading and talking about their own books
- keep a reading journal to record title, author, thoughts, feelings, memories and opinions of text.

Continue to assess during independent reading. This usually takes the form of a *reading conference*.

All of the information gathered during independent reading conferences helps to decide the purposes for shared and guided reading instruction.

A form of independent reading is *paired* or *partner reading*.

When two students read together without teacher assistance, they are able to help each other. Students can be paired with peers, or with older or younger students.

Responding to reading

After students have had experience with an interesting text through read aloud, shared reading, guided reading, book or literature group or independent reading, they should be provided with opportunities to respond to what they have read.

Well-planned response activities help students to:
- deepen understanding of reading material
- share insights
- seek clarification
- offer new information learned
- expand thinking
- create pictures in their minds based on reading
- analyze, compare and evaluate.

Some ways students might respond to reading are:
- retelling, both orally and in writing (*Read and Retell*, Cambourne & Brown, 1987)
- reader's theater
- dramatizing
- writing in a reading response journal (*In the Middle*, Atwell, 1987)
- talking
- choosing a relevant graphic organizer or semantic web to represent the ideas and structure of the text.

School .... Class ....
Name .... Term ....

Reading band G

Reading strategies

Reads manuals and literature of varying complexity. Interprets simple maps, tables and graphs in the context of discursive text. Makes generalizations and draws conclusions from reading. Reads at different speeds, using scanning, skim-reading or careful reading as appropriate.

Responses

Supports argument or opinion by reference to evidence presented in sources outside text. Compares information from different sources. Identifies opposing points of view and main and supporting arguments in text. Comments on cohesiveness of text as a whole. Discusses and writes about author's bias and technique. In writing, offers critical opinion or analysis of reading materials. Distils and links ideas from complex sentences and paragraphs.

Interests and attitudes

Reads widely for pleasure, for interest or for learning.

Comment

Reading band H

Reading strategies

Compiles own list of needed references, using bibliographies and literature-search techniques. Interprets material at different levels of meaning. Forms generalizations about a range of genres, including myth, short story. Lists a wide variety of sources read for specific learning tasks.

Responses

Identifies plot and subplot. Identifies allegory. Formulates hypothetical questions about a subject, based on prior reading. Compares and offers critical analysis of materials presented in the media. Extracts ideas embedded in complex passages of text. Displays critical opinion and analysis in written reports of reading. Identifies different authors' points of view on a topic. Reformulates a task in the light of available reading resources. Questions and reflects on issues encountered in texts. Shows understanding by being able to adopt an alternative point of view to the author's. Discusses styles used by different authors.

Comment

Reading band I

Reading strategies

Examines situational meaning of text. Explores a range of meaning dependent on the combination of influences of writer, reader and situation.

Responses

Explains textual innuendo and undertone. Interprets analogy, allegory and parable in text. Identifies and explains deeper significance in text. Defends each interpretation of text. Discusses and writes about author's bias. Analyzes cohesiveness of text as a whole.

Comment

Suggested new indicators

Reading Writing Speaking and listening

A B C D E F G H I

READING band

Is skillful in analyzing and interpreting own response to reading.
Can respond to a wide range of text styles.

Contexts for observation: Curriculum focus

Discussion of issues at *reading circles* provides opportunities for students to share significant issues. These should then be explored through texts that focus on interpretation, authors' bias, innuendo and undertone.

Literature response portfolios provide a vehicle for students to critically and analytically consider text. Negotiated criteria will determine the direction student responses take. These criteria should be listed in the student's portfolio.

Discussion with students about *text cohesion* will allow the teacher to observe how well they interpret text and justify decisions. Students' understanding regarding the cultural milieu of novels may be elicited here.

A *drama workshop*, in which students rehearse and revise their interpretations of a scene from a play, provides an occasion for observing the way they articulate and defend their perceptions of a text.

Writing and *discussion* reveal students' understandings about the way a literary work may be both a particular story and a more general illumination of aspects of human life.

Close analysis of a selected passage and the ways in which it relates to and illuminates the whole work will show students' understanding of structural and metaphoric cohesion in the text.

School .... Class ....
Name.. Term ....

Reading band H

Reading strategies

Compiles own list of needed references, using bibliographies and literature-search techniques. Interprets material at different levels of meaning. Forms generalizations about a range of genres, including myth, short story. Lists a wide variety of sources read for specific learning tasks.

Responses

Identifies plot and subplot. Identifies allegory. Formulates hypothetical questions about a subject, based on prior reading. Compares and offers critical analysis of materials presented in the media. Extracts ideas embedded in complex passages of text. Displays critical opinion and analysis in written reports of reading. Identifies different authors' points of view on a topic. Reformulates a task in the light of available reading resources. Questions and reflects on issues encountered in texts. Shows understanding by being able to adopt an alternative point of view to the author's. Discusses styles used by different authors.

Comment

Reading band I

Reading strategies

Examines situational meaning of text. Explores a range of meaning dependent on the combination of influences of writer, reader and situation.

Responses

Explains textual innuendo and undertone. Interprets analogy, allegory and parable in text. Identifies and explains deeper significance in text. Defends each interpretation of text. Discusses and writes about author's bias. Analyzes cohesiveness of text as a whole.

Comment

Suggested new indicators

Speaking and listening

Writing

Reading

A B C D E F G H **I**

Chapter 6

Writing profile records

WRITING band

Knows that writing says something.
Is curious about environmental print.
Is starting to see patterns.

Contexts for observation: Curriculum focus

Writing to students

Modeled writing

During *modeled writing* sessions the teacher thinks aloud and writes to show students how to make decisions about what to write and how to write by modeling:

- how oral language can be written down
- concepts of print, words and letters, spaces, directionality, left to right, top to bottom, punctuation
- composing a message, holding the idea and rereading each time something new is added.

Modeled writing can be used in association with read aloud and shared reading with the teacher noting predictions, unfolding events and conclusions.

Writing with students

Shared and interactive writing

Shared writing, where the adult or teacher scribes for a group, is an approach where joint composition takes place.

Shared writing is often an outcome of:
- a shared experience such as a class trip
- compiling class news reports
- writing known nursery rhymes as students watch and join in
- brainstorming class instructions for making things or working at activity areas in the classroom.

Interactive writing is a deliberate, planned activity where the teacher helps children acquire problem solving strategies to use when they write for themselves. Children work as a group with the teacher, to compose and write the message.

Interactive writing at this stage — in Kindergarten — is often the 'mini-lesson' that takes place at the start of the writing workshop.

The teaching at this emergent stage is designed to focus on the developing early reading and writing behaviors:
- directional movement and one-to-one matching
- concepts of letters, words and sentences
- letter knowledge
- familiarity with frequently encountered words (high-frequency and 'anchor' words)
- rereading and predicting strategies.

Writing by students

Independent writing

By planning for *independent writing* every day, the teacher gives the students opportunities to apply recently demonstrated techniques and strategies.

As the students write, observe how they solve problems and use what they know about writing. Nudge and coach students into using their full capabilities.

Encourage writing by providing:
- a developing word wall which students use as a resource when they write
- a range of appropriate paper
- a range of writing equipment
- alphabet cards and charts
- magnetic letters for word making and solving
- charts of daily modeled, shared and interactive writing to which they can refer
- books (during shared reading and read aloud) that feature rhyme, rhythm and repetition.

Knowledge of letters, sounds and words

In a balanced literacy program students learn about and practice word making (in writing) and word solving (in reading) strategies.

The focus across the approaches at this stage of development will be on:
- learning about letters and sounds — phonemic awareness
- learning words by analogy — for example, a student who knows ball and sack may take the onset b and the rhyme ack and make back
- using environmental print from the classroom to help build a growing 'writing' vocabulary.

School .... Class ....

Name.. Term ....

Writing band A

What the writer does

Uses writing implement to make marks on paper. Explains the meaning of marks (word, sentence, writing, letter). Copies 'words' from signs in immediate environment. 'Reads', understands and explains own 'writing'.

What the writing shows

Understanding of the difference between picture and print. Use of some recognizable symbols found in writing.

Use of writing

Comments on signs and other symbols in immediate environment. Uses a mixture of drawings and 'writing' to convey and support an idea.

Comment

Writing band B

What the writer does

Reproduces words from signs and other sources in immediate environment. Holds pencil/pen using satisfactory grip. Uses preferred hand consistently for writing. Attempts to put 'words' in 'sentence' format. 'Writes' a simple message. Uses sound–symbol linkages. 'Captions' or 'labels' drawings.

What the writing shows

Use of vocabulary of print (letters, words, question marks, etc.). Use of letters of the alphabet and other conventional symbols. Use of letters in groups to form words. Placing of spaces between groups of 'letters'. Knowledge that writing moves from left to right in lines from top to bottom of page.

Use of writing

Writes own name.

Interests and attitudes

Understands that writing is talk written down.

Comment

Suggested new indicators

Speaking and listening   Writing   Reading

A B C D E F G H I

Contexts for observation: Curriculum focus

Writing to students
Modeled writing
During *modeled writing* show, through thinking aloud and writing, how to:
- make a choice about what to write
- brainstorm around an idea
- compose a written message
- innovate on a familiar text structure — for example from a poem or rhyme
- write information, showing how information texts are different from narrative texts
- use personal experiences as a source of writing.

Writing with students
Shared writing
During *shared writing*, scribe for the class or groups of students as they compose:
- messages to others — shopping lists, telephone messages
- letters, or greetings
- instructions to make or do things
- recounts of experiences or procedures
- reflections about something that has been read during read aloud, shared reading or independent reading sessions.

Interactive writing
Students at the emergent level need to rehearse their story or message before they write, deciding which words to use and learning to hold the message in their heads.

The focus of *interactive writing* should be to help students develop understandings that:
- the message is in the print
- print carries a constant message
- print follows conventions — left to right and top to bottom
- a word is a unit of print with space at either side
- a sentence consists of several words
- words have letters which represent sound segments
- they should hear and represent beginnings and endings of words as they write — especially beginning and ending consonants
- a letter can represent a range of sounds
- words can rhyme and have similar letter patterns
- words can be broken into chunks.

Writing by students
Independent writing
During *independent writing* time, students will be increasingly able to:
- generate longer pieces of writing so they may use and repeat known words or letter patterns, frequently using letters from their own names
- use larger combinations of letters to represent known words — 2 or 3 letters for a whole word
- read back their own writing
- use writing to convey a message
- write spontaneously for themselves or for a wider audience
- employ some revision strategies such as crossing out, or inserting words
- use drawing to add to a written message, in order to provide more information.

School .... Class ....

Name .... Term ....

	Comment
Writing band A **What the writer does** Uses writing implement to make marks on paper. Explains the meaning of marks (word, sentence, writing, letter). Copies 'words' from signs in immediate environment. 'Reads', understands and explains own 'writing'. **What the writing shows** Understanding of the difference between picture and print. Use of some recognizable symbols found in writing. **Use of writing** Comments on signs and other symbols in immediate environment. Uses a mixture of drawings and 'writing' to convey and support an idea.	
Writing band B **What the writer does** Reproduces words from signs and other sources in immediate environment. Holds pencil/pen using satisfactory grip. Uses preferred hand consistently for writing. Attempts to put 'words' in 'sentence' format. 'Writes' a simple message. Uses sound–symbol linkages. 'Captions' or 'labels' drawings. **What the writing shows** Use of vocabulary of print (letters, words, question marks, etc.). Use of letters of the alphabet and other conventional symbols. Use of letters in groups to form words. Placing of spaces between groups of 'letters'. Knowledge that writing moves from left to right in lines from top to bottom of page. **Use of writing** Writes own name. **Interests and attitudes** Understands that writing is talk written down.	
Writing band C **What the writer does** Commences writing without assistance. Has a personalized handwriting style that meets most handwriting needs. Checks written work by reading it aloud. Sounds out words as an aid to spelling. **What the writing shows** Legible writing with recognizable words. Words put together in sentence format. Words written in a logical order to make a sentence that can be read. Upper and lower case letters used conventionally. Written sentences that can be understood by an adult. **Use of writing** Sentences convey message on one topic. Uses 'I' in writing. Writes about feelings, judgment or direct experience. Creates characters from experience and immediate environment.	

Suggested new indicators

Speaking and listening

Writing

Reading

I H G F E D C B A

WRITING band

Now says something in own writing.
Is writing own sentences.
Is taking an interest in appearance of writing.

Contexts for observation: Curriculum focus

Writing to students

Modeled writing

Students need to see that writing is a natural way of communicating, and that written language is ordered in a planned way.

When teachers use a chart or OHP to show students how they go about writing, they:

- demonstrate the thinking and planning, composing and revising, and correcting involved in writing
- can model a range of writing genres, including the early genres of observation and comment, recount and 'how to' or instructional writing
- show children how to revise writing, focusing on making the meaning clear.

Writing with students

Shared writing

Shared writing (often called *language experience*) can be a format for teachers, or other adults, to scribe for students while they jointly compose texts, focusing on:

- correct ordering so the text has structure (beginning, middle, end) and meaning
- innovations on familiar texts
- a class diary during a theme or topic study
- reports following an investigation in Math or Science.

Interactive writing

By being involved in *interactive writing*, students will have learned how to brainstorm ideas and compose simple messages.

They now need experience in being involved in the creation of longer texts, often over the course of several days.

The interactive writing session may focus on:

- how to start the message or story
- gathering the facts to include in the piece
- constructing and continually rereading longer texts
- introducing key words such as when, where, what and how
- introducing words made by using the students' growing knowledge of onset and rhyme
- helping students hear sounds in the middle of words, and represent them with the correct letters.

Writing by students

Independent writing

The daily writing workshop session should include a focus session, time for *independent writing* and revising, as well as time for conferences and sharing time. Students should publish their writing often.

Teachers' conferences with students may focus on:

- control over meaning and syntax
- clarity of content and purpose
- revision strategies the student is developing
- encouraging a willingness to take risks, to 'have-a-go'
- the student's increasing knowledge of vocabulary
- helping the student to develop a sense of audience
- word study and spelling.

School .... Class ....

Name.. Term ....

	Comment
Writing band B **What the writer does** Reproduces words from signs and other sources in immediate environment. Holds pencil/pen using satisfactory grip. Uses preferred hand consistently for writing. Attempts to put 'words' in 'sentence' format. 'Writes' a simple message. Uses sound–symbol linkages. 'Captions' or 'labels' drawings. **What the writing shows** Use of vocabulary of print (letters, words, question marks, etc.). Use of letters of the alphabet and other conventional symbols. Use of letters in groups to form words. Placing of spaces between groups of 'letters'. Knowledge that writing moves from left to right in lines from top to bottom of page. **Use of writing** Writes own name. **Interests and attitudes** Understands that writing is talk written down.	
Writing band C **What the writer does** Commences writing without assistance. Has a personalized handwriting style that meets most handwriting needs. Checks written work by reading it aloud. Sounds out words as an aid to spelling. **What the writing shows** Legible writing with recognizable words. Words put together in sentence format. Words written in a logical order to make a sentence that can be read. Upper and lower case letters used conventionally. Written sentences that can be understood by an adult. **Use of writing** Sentences convey message on one topic. Uses 'I' in writing. Writes about feelings, judgment or direct experience. Creates characters from experience and immediate environment.	
Writing band D **What the writer does** Marks most common words with incorrect spelling when editing writing. Uses ideas, themes and structure from books in writing. Uses concepts of order and time in writing. Reads, rereads and revises own written work. Uses everyday words in appropriate written context. **What the writing shows** Punctuation used conventionally. Conventional spelling used most of the time; spelling showing recall of visual patterns. Stories that can be read, understood and retold by classmates. Several sentences constructed on one topic in a logical order. A smooth connection of ideas. Beginning, middle and end in narrative writing. **Use of writing** Writes stories containing characters from outside personal environment. Writes with ease on most matters of personal experience. Writes on a variety of topics. Writes personal anecdotes and letters to friends. Writes for a known audience. Uses a range of written forms — poems, letters, journals, logs, etc.	

Suggested new indicators

Speaking and listening
Writing
Reading

A B C D E F G H I

WRITING band D

Can write own stories.
Changes words and spelling until satisfied with the result.

Contexts for observation: Curriculum focus

Speaking and listening
Writing
Reading
A B C D E F G H I

Writing to students

Modeled writing

Modeled writing can be a session with the class or small groups, brought together for specific purposes. New concepts and genres can be modeled for students several times before they try it for themselves.

Use modeled writing to demonstrate to students how to:

- go about choosing a topic
- take, organize and keep notes
- write in curriculum areas — Math, Science and Social Studies
- model unfamiliar text forms such as recount, procedure, description, report, summary, and both persuasive and informational text.

Writing with students

As students develop as writers, they should be provided with the opportunity to participate in shared situations.

Shared and assisted writing

Shared writing and *assisted writing* involve working with a writing buddy or a conference partner, or joint publishing opportunities.

During shared writing teachers and students may:

- construct a new form of writing together
- record activities or information with a group

- record daily events, including news
- jointly write various forms of functional print — timetables, schedules, rosters, rules, vocabulary charts.

Assisted writing is sometimes called *guided writing*. When bringing a small group of students with similar needs together for assisted writing, the teacher uses prompts to initiate problem solving, enabling students to accomplish writing tasks they would not be able to do on their own. Guide students in learning how to use skills, strategies and facts that they know in writing.

Assisted writing is a progression from interactive writing, in that the student does the composing and the writing, but with teacher and group support.

Peer partnerships or writing buddies

Students may be paired, enabling an older or more accomplished writer to work collaboratively with another student on a piece of writing. Both participate in the writing process, producing a joint piece of writing.

Publishing partnerships

Students can form small groups to jointly publish a piece of writing. They may choose a piece drafted by one of the group and work together, to revise, correct and publish the piece.

Over some weeks, it is possible for each student in a group to take a draft to publishing using this group publishing approach, learning that the purpose and audience dictate the form that writing takes.

Writing by students

Independent writing

Writing increasingly becomes a product of new learning experiences, and a tool to use in learning.

Students should engage in a wide variety of writing experiences including:

- content area procedure and report writing
- reflective writing associated with writing
- note-taking and the organization and presentation of information
- learning journals kept for content area learning — Math and Science journals
- letters written to request information, or to share new learning
- on-line writing, using e-mail
- poetry and verse writing
- recipes, instructions and other procedural texts.

Through these experiences, they learn as writers to:

- write often for — and communicate with — a wide audience
- write in a range of different genres
- write to entertain, and inform
- draw on an increasingly wider range of resources when they plan to write
- modify, tighten and polish their writing to better reach their readers
- revise their writing, monitoring and clarifying the meaning, and choosing words appropriate to the text
- use journals to record thoughts and responses to independent reading.

Editing, proofreading and correcting spelling development

Students need to be taught the skills necessary to proofread, edit and correct their own and other students' writing.

A useful routine is to schedule a time toward the end of each day's writing workshop where the teacher, using his or her own writing or that of students on a chart or OHP transparency, models the skills necessary to accurately proofread and correct. A proofreading code similar to that used by publishers can be introduced, or the class can make their own.

Each day students get into the habit of identifying things — words, capital letters, punctuation and grammar — that need 'fixing up'. This self-correction process can involve teaching students how to:

- change what has been written
- reread to check for conventional spelling and grammar
- cross out and insert words, phrases and sentences
- use the editor (cut and paste) and spell checker in a computer.

A 'have-a-try' process should be set up, with students learning to:

- write a problem word two or three times and identify the one which looks right
- check their try using a word wall, word bank or dictionary
- write the word again, and then use 'look, say, cover, write, check'
- write the word from memory.

The correction can be made to the writing, and the newly mastered word written by the students in their personal spelling books or word banks.

Writing profile record

School .... Class ....

Name .... Term ....

Writing band C

Comment

What the writer does
Commences writing without assistance. Has a personalized handwriting style that meets most handwriting needs. Checks written work by reading it aloud. Sounds out words as an aid to spelling.

What the writing shows
Legible writing with recognizable words. Words put together in sentence format. Words written in a logical order to make a sentence that can be read. Upper and lower case letters used conventionally. Written sentences that can be understood by an adult.

Use of writing
Sentences convey message on one topic. Uses 'I' in writing. Writes about feelings, judgment or direct experience. Creates characters from experience and immediate environment.

Writing band D

Comment

What the writer does
Marks most common words with incorrect spelling when editing writing. Uses ideas, themes and structure from books in writing. Uses concepts of order and time in writing. Reads, rereads and revises own written work. Uses everyday words in appropriate written context.

What the writing shows
Punctuation used conventionally. Conventional spelling used most of the time; spelling showing recall of visual patterns. Stories that can be read, understood and retold by classmates. Several sentences constructed on one topic in a logical order. A smooth connection of ideas. Beginning, middle and end in narrative writing.

Use of writing
Writes stories containing characters from outside personal environment. Writes with ease on most matters of personal experience. Writes on a variety of topics. Writes personal anecdotes and letters to friends. Writes for a known audience. Uses a range of written forms — poems, letters, journals, logs, etc.

Writing band E

Comment

What the writer does
Edits work to a point where others can read it; corrects common spelling errors, punctuation and grammatical errors. Develops ideas into paragraphs. Uses a dictionary, thesaurus or word-checker to extend and check vocabulary for writing. Uses vivid, specific language.

What the writing shows
Sentences with ideas that flow. Paragraphs with a cohesive structure. Ability to present relationships and to argue or persuade. Messages in expository and argumentative writing identifiable by others, although some information may be omitted. Brief passages written with clear meaning, accuracy of spelling and apt punctuation. Appropriate shifts from first to third person in writing. Consistent use of the correct tense. Appropriate vocabulary for familiar audiences such as peers, younger children or adults, with only occasional inappropriate word choice. Compound sentences, using conjunctions. Variations of letters, print styles or fonts. A print style appropriate to task and a consistent handwriting style.

Use of writing
Writes a properly sequenced text with a convincing setting. Creates characters from imagination.

Suggested new indicators

WRITING band

Can plan, organize and polish writing.
Writes in paragraphs.
Uses vocabulary and grammar suited to topic.
Can write convincing stories.

Contexts for observation: Curriculum focus

Writing to and with students

Modeled and shared writing

In *modeled writing* the teacher, using a large chart or an OHP, shows students how they go about:

* forming intentions
* drafting and revising
* proofreading and correcting, and publishing.

These demonstrations of the writing process in action can lead to shared writing, where the students join in the process, but the teacher continues to scribe for the group.

Some of the purposes for modeled and shared writing may include modeling how a writer:

* selects relevant information from many sources before writing
* transfers information from reading to writing by taking notes
* brainstorms ideas, and uses graphic organizers to sort out ideas and thoughts
* constantly rereads and revises writing while drafting, or revises after drafting
* reorders text to clarify meaning.

Interactive writing

By this stage (band E) of student's development, the literacy demonstrations involved in *interactive writing* may not be necessary. However, small groups may still be brought together to practice writing two- and three-sentence messages that demonstrate they are able to control a specific genre and use punctuation to support meaning.

Writing with students

Writing workshop

During the daily *writing workshop*, establish a predictable routine working with students as a class, in small groups and as individuals. The routine may be:

* *a focus session* (or 'mini-lesson'), where the teacher, through reading or writing, models and articulates the writing process and the skills to enable writing development
* *writing time*, where students write for long periods of time in their notebooks, drafting or revising pieces of writing, or taking a selected piece through to publishing
* *conference time*, where the teacher meets with individuals, or a small group, assisting students to clarify purpose, and meaning
* *proofreading and correcting time*, which may include a time specifically devoted to ensuring that any text

that is to be read by others is as correct as the writer can make it — either individually or with assistance.

The student's approach should always be: 'How can I make my writing ready for the readers?'.

Sharing time

This is time when students share their writing by reading to the class or group.

By inviting questions and feedback, students learn from each other and develop a growing sense of audience. It helps if the teacher models the sort of feedback that is useful.

Publishing

Publishing means to make public. This can be done by students:

* reading their writing to a group, or class
* showing or displaying the work
* working in a group to type, illustrate and circulate a piece
* together publishing class or group writing in book format.

Writing by students

The focus of the writing workshops planned at this level of development may be to enable students to:

* plan and write both narrative and informational (expository or non-fiction) texts
* adapt their writing to suit specific purposes
* use and discuss features of basic text types:
    - to inform and understand (reports, summaries, graphs and charts, tables, letters and simple directions)
    - to respond and interpret (original imaginative texts, stories and narratives)
    - to analyze and evaluate (note-taking and concept webs, editorials and reviews)
    - to interact (personal letters, notes, cards, e-mails).

Editing, proofreading and correcting for publishing

The competencies that students should demonstrate as they learn to write are:

* to use an organizational format that reflects a beginning, middle and end
* to develop an idea within a brief text
* to learn and use the writing process (form intentions, draft and revise, correct and publish)
* to determine the intended audience before writing
* to spell accurately, and control syntax and tense.

Writing band D
What the writer does
Marks most common words with incorrect spelling when editing writing. Uses ideas, themes and structure from books in writing. Uses concepts of order and time in writing. Reads, rereads and revises own written work. Uses everyday words in appropriate written context.

What the writing shows
Punctuation used conventionally. Conventional spelling used most of the time; spelling showing recall of visual patterns. Stories that can be read, understood and retold by classmates. Several sentences constructed on one topic in a logical order. A smooth connection of ideas. Beginning, middle and end in narrative writing.

Use of writing
Writes stories containing characters from outside personal environment. Writes with ease on most matters of personal experience. Writes on a variety of topics. Writes personal anecdotes and letters to friends. Writes for a known audience. Uses a range of written forms — poems, letters, journals, logs, etc.

Comment

Writing band E
What the writer does
Edits work to a point where others can read it; corrects common spelling errors, punctuation and grammatical errors. Develops ideas into paragraphs. Uses a dictionary, thesaurus or word-checker to extend and check vocabulary for writing. Uses vivid, specific language.

What the writing shows
Sentences with ideas that flow. Paragraphs with a cohesive structure. Ability to present relationships and to argue or persuade. Messages in expository and argumentative writing identifiable by others, although some information may be omitted. Brief passages written with clear meaning, accuracy of spelling and apt punctuation. Appropriate shifts from first to third person in writing. Consistent use of the correct tense. Appropriate vocabulary for familiar audiences such as peers, younger children or adults, with only occasional inappropriate word choice. Compound sentences, using conjunctions. Variations of letters, print styles or fonts. A print style appropriate to task and a consistent handwriting style.

Use of writing
Writes a properly sequenced text with a convincing setting. Creates characters from imagination.

Comment

Writing band F
What the writer does
Writes sentences in different forms: statement, question, command, explanation. Writes paragraphs to develop logical sequence of ideas. Corrects most spelling, punctuation and grammatical errors in editing others' written work. Consults available sources to improve or enhance writing. Joins letters, using linkages where appropriate, to form personal handwriting style.

What the writing shows
Narratives containing introduction, complication and resolution in a logical order. Longer descriptions and narratives developed coherently. Use of both active and passive voice. A range of vocabulary and grammatical structures. Complex sentences — principal and subordinate clauses. Higher level writing skills in areas of special interest. Understanding of the difference between narrative and other forms of writing.

Use of writing
Completes standard forms requiring personal information. Makes appropriate use of narrative and other forms of writing.

Comment

Suggested new indicators

WRITING band

Can describe things well.
Can skillfully write and tell a story or describe phenomena.
Now has skills to improve writing.

Contexts for observation: Curriculum focus

Writing to and with students

During *modeled* and *shared writing* teachers may introduce and consolidate important aspects of writing in all curriculum areas. Include important writing understandings used in Mathematics, Social Studies and Science, and how to transmit information, by:

- taking notes and recording data (this can be directly linked with read aloud and shared reading)
- stating a main idea and supporting it with facts and details
- producing clear, well-organized and well-developed explanations, reports, accounts and directions.

Over time, modeled and shared writing time may be used to introduce and demonstrate to students the following forms of writing: short reports, brief summaries, graphs and charts, concept maps and graphic organizers, simple outlines, letters and directions.

Other understandings include:

- how to respond to and express themselves in imaginative texts — including stories, poems, folktales and fables, plays, film and video production
- how to critically analyze and evaluate ideas, information and expression — including persuasive essays, editorials, reviews of movies and books, reports and advertisements
- how to establish, maintain and enhance personal relationships.

Teachers may model other forms of writing, including friendly notes, letters and cards to friends and relatives, sending pen letters or e-mails, and keeping personal journals.

Writing with students

Writing workshop

The role for teachers during daily *writing workshops* is to help students with the following key understandings.

- Writing is a craft involving manipulating words and information to match the writer's intended meaning.
- Writing involves revising, because a writer wants the information to be accurate. This means making good choices about what should stay and what can be discarded from a draft.

The teaching involves reading and listening to the writing of others — published authors and classmates — as well as conferences, conducted regularly by the teacher or by classmates, that focus on meaning, content, form and clarity.

Donald Graves (1983) says teachers use 'temporary structures during the conference process with students' writing'. These conference structure elements are:

- *be predictable* — students should be able to predict what will happen in a conference
- *be focused* — on no more than one or two features of the piece
- *demonstrate solutions* — teachers show, rather than tell the student what to do
- *reverse roles* — students should be free to initiate comments and questions
- *have a growing common language* — to discuss the process and content of subjects
- *be playful* — there may be a combination of experimentation, discovery and humour.

Writing by students

When students demonstrate that they use writing for information and understanding, they should be able to:

- use at least three sources of information
- take notes to record and organize relevant data
- compare and contrast ideas and information from various sources
- maintain a portfolio with various writing genres.

Provide many opportunities for students to read and write imaginary texts, such as stories, poems, songs and plays, to write interpretive and imaginative essays and to respond to literature, making connections to personal experiences.

Students need to be able to use writing to gather, sort and evaluate information, ideas and experiences, using:

- note-taking, graphic organizers and mapping to plan and organize writing
- precise, appropriate vocabulary in writing analysis and evaluation
- information and ideas from across subject areas and personal experiences to form and express opinions and judgments.

Writing to interact socially can be encouraged through letters, cards, notes and e-mail, while personal and interactive journals can be kept to document learning.

Editing, proofreading and correcting for publishing

Proofreading needs to be taught. It is a special kind of reading that demands slowing down and close attention to detail, and may include:

- circling words that a student is unsure of, and using resources such as a spelling notebook, 'have-a-go' sheet, word walls, dictionary, thesaurus, computer spell-check or peers to enable correction
- demonstration by both teacher and students, on an OHP, of useful proofreading techniques.

Writing profile record

School .... Class ....

Name.. Term ....

Speaking and listening

Reading   **Writing**

A B C D E **F** G H I

Writing band E

What the writer does

Edits work to a point where others can read it; corrects common spelling errors, punctuation and grammatical errors. Develops ideas into paragraphs. Uses a dictionary, thesaurus or word-checker to extend and check vocabulary for writing. Uses vivid, specific language.

What the writing shows

Sentences with ideas that flow. Paragraphs with a cohesive structure. Ability to present relationships and to argue or persuade. Messages in expository and argumentative writing identifiable by others, although some information may be omitted. Brief passages written with clear meaning, accuracy of spelling and apt punctuation. Appropriate shifts from first to third person in writing. Consistent use of the correct tense. Appropriate vocabulary for familiar audiences such as peers, younger children or adults, with only occasional inappropriate word choice. Compound sentences, using conjunctions. Variations of letters, print styles or fonts. A print style appropriate to task and a consistent handwriting style.

Use of writing

Writes a properly sequenced text with a convincing setting. Creates characters from imagination.

Comment

Writing band F

What the writer does

Writes sentences in different forms: statement, question, command, explanation. Writes paragraphs to develop logical sequence of ideas. Corrects most spelling, punctuation and grammatical errors in editing others' written work. Consults available sources to improve or enhance writing. Joins letters, using linkages where appropriate, to form personal handwriting style.

What the writing shows

Narratives containing introduction, complication and resolution in a logical order. Longer descriptions and narratives developed coherently. Use of both active and passive voice. A range of vocabulary and grammatical structures. Complex sentences — principal and subordinate clauses. Higher level writing skills in areas of special interest. Understanding of the difference between narrative and other forms of writing.

Use of writing

Completes standard forms requiring personal information. Makes appropriate use of narrative and other forms of writing.

Comment

Writing band G

What the writer does

Writes in narrative, expository and argumentative styles. Uses a range of writing styles effectively and appropriately for purpose, situation and audience. Uses a range of vocabulary effectively and appropriately for purpose, situation and audience. Edits work to improve the smooth flow of ideas and reorganizes work to make it more readable. Replaces words and sentences during revision of written work. Changes sequence of ideas, adds new ideas during revision.

What the writing shows

Main and supporting ideas presented clearly. Correct format for letters, invitations. Figurative language, such as simile, for descriptive purposes.

Use of writing

Shows a range of styles — written conversations, poems, plays, journals. Writes formal and social letters and distinguishes between the purposes of each. Adapts writing to demands of task. Completes complex forms that seek detailed biographical and related information.

Comment

Suggested new indicators

WRITING band G

Uses rich vocabulary, and writing style depends on topic, purpose, and audience.
Produces lively and colorful writing.
Can do major revision of writing.

Contexts for observation: Curriculum focus

Writing to and with students

At this stage of development, students are independent writers. But teachers need to provide guidance to enable them to approach more complex and demanding writing tasks.

Modeled and shared writing can and should continue to be used during the writing workshop, but flexible group arrangements need to be considered to enable the needs of all students to be met, so the modeled and shared writing can take place with individuals, pairs, small groups or the whole class.

The demands of the content areas mean that students need to be shown how information from a variety of sources is incorporated into writing.

At this stage of writing development, students should be familiar with, and have the opportunity to use:

- reports, summaries, graphs and charts, instructions and directions, business letters, news articles and outlines
- narratives, poems, songs, plays and literature responses
- persuasive essays, book and movie reviews, editorials in class or school newspapers
- friendly letters, notes and cards, personal journals and diaries, and e-mails.

These can all be the focus for modeled and shared writing.

Fairy Tale	Beginning Words	Good Characters	Evil Character	Magic	Ending Words
Cinderella	Once upon a time...	• Cinderella • Prince • Fairy Godmother	• the mother • ...psister	Magic Wand turned: pumpkin into a coach, horse into a coachman, dog into a footman, mice into horses, rags into gown, shoes into slippers	And they lived happily ever after.
Rapunzel	Long ago...	• Rapunzel • the prince	• the sorceress	Rapunzel's tears restored the Prince's eyesight.	There they lived a long life, happy and content.
Snow White	Long ago,...	• Snow White • the Seven Dwarfs • the prince	• the Queen, her stepmother	Magic Mirror, poisoned apple that made her sleep	...where they lived happily ever after.
Jack and the Beanstalk	There was once upon a time...	• Jack • Jack's mother	• the giant	Magic beans, Hen that laid golden eggs, Golden harp that sang	...and they lived happily ever after.
Rumpelstiltskin	Once there was...	• the miller's daughter	• the King • Rumpelstiltskin	Spinning straw into gold, riding on a spoon	And that was the end of Rumpelstiltskin.
The Twelve Dancing Princesses	Come a little closer...	• the King • the soldier	• the twelve Princesses	the invisible cloak, the bed that sank into the earth, trees with silver, gold and diamond leaves	...danced until three o'clock in the morning.
Sleeping Beauty	In a kingdom long ago...	• the King and Queen • the Prince • the good fairies	• the evil fairy	Magic wands that gave the princess gifts, a spindle that put the princess to sleep	And the good fairy came to watch over them, so they never fell into...

Writing with students

Competent writers who have been working in *process writing* classrooms for a number of years should understand the writing process. The teacher's role is to continually support, guide and coach writers to independence and self-reliance.

The writing process, whether in a Language Arts, Mathematics, Science or Social Studies class, should enable students to take ideas from incubation to publishing. They should have the opportunity each day to:

- form intentions:
  - clarifying the purpose
  - gathering information
  - testing ideas about content and form
  - trying to establish an audience for the writing
- compose and draft:
  - revising and reorganizing

- clarifying and shaping meaning until the intention and form becomes clear
- correct and proofread:
  - making the necessary modifications to the surface features so that all conventions are used correctly and the reader gets the clear message
- publish, share and reflect:
  - providing the writer with responses from their own readers.

Writing by students

Writing in school should be used in all subjects of the curriculum to increase writing ability. It should cover as many forms and kinds of writing as possible and appropriate, and be related to the world outside schools.

Because of the focus on meaning, teachers should model, and encourage in conferences that 'clarification of meaning is the pivot of revision in writing' (*Dancing with the Pen*, Department of Education, New Zealand, 1996).

At the completion of a draft, the student may have:

- added and clarified information
- reordered parts of the text
- deleted or replaced words and phrases.

The student should also:

- be satisfied with the structure of the writing
- see that readers understand the intended message
- know that drafting and revision are concerned with meaning
- check as far as possible to see if facts are correct
- know that as far as possible surface conventions have been attended to and corrected.

This can all be achieved through *conferences* — talking in groups, in pairs and with the teacher. Sharing and talking are important ways for writers to clarify meaning.

Proofreading and correcting for publishing

'Proofreading is a habit that all writers need to develop, because the writing process involves so many things to think about, that it is easy to make mistakes while writing' (Snowball & Bolton, 1999).

Proofreading should be a daily habit, and at this level of development the teacher may use the following techniques.

- Demonstrate how proofreading is done — by the teacher or a student, using writing enlarged on a chart or an OHP.
- Work with individuals in a proofreading conference.
- Develop with students a proofreading code or system known and understood by all (e.g. circle doubtful words and put a check over the letters they are sure are right).
- Use 'try-it-out' or 'have-a-go' sheets that encourage students to try a word more than one way, and then select the most likely fit.
- Spell-check computer programs — when using on- and off-line computer programs students should be encouraged to spell-check.
- Use all available resources — dictionaries, word books, word lists, environmental print, other books and people.

As in reading, students should be shown how and encouraged to monitor their own writing by asking themselves if the writing:

- makes sense (semantically correct)
- sounds right (syntactically correct)
- looks right (graphophonically correct).

School .... Class ....
Name.. Term ....

	Comment
## Writing band F ### What the writer does Writes sentences in different forms: statement, question, command, explanation. Writes paragraphs to develop logical sequence of ideas. Corrects most spelling, punctuation and grammatical errors in editing others' written work. Consults available sources to improve or enhance writing. Joins letters, using linkages where appropriate, to form personal handwriting style. ### What the writing shows Narratives containing introduction, complication and resolution in a logical order. Longer descriptions and narratives developed coherently. Use of both active and passive voice. A range of vocabulary and grammatical structures. Complex sentences — principal and subordinate clauses. Higher level writing skills in areas of special interest. Understanding of the difference between narrative and other forms of writing. ### Use of writing Completes standard forms requiring personal information. Makes appropriate use of narrative and other forms of writing.	
## Writing band G ### What the writer does Writes in narrative, expository and argumentative styles. Uses a range of writing styles effectively and appropriately for purpose, situation and audience. Uses a range of vocabulary effectively and appropriately for purpose, situation and audience. Edits work to improve the smooth flow of ideas and reorganizes work to make it more readable. Replaces words and sentences during revision of written work. Changes sequence of ideas, adds new ideas during revision. ### What the writing shows Main and supporting ideas presented clearly. Correct format for letters, invitations. Figurative language, such as simile, for descriptive purposes. ### Use of writing Shows a range of styles — written conversations, poems, plays, journals. Writes formal and social letters and distinguishes between the purposes of each. Adapts writing to demands of task. Completes complex forms that seek detailed biographical and related information.	
## Writing band H ### What the writer does Edits and revises own work to enhance effect of vocabulary, text organization and layout. Edits and revises others' writing, improving presentation and structure without losing meaning or message. ### What the writing shows Meaning expressed precisely. Organization and layout of written text accurate and appropriate for purpose, situation and audience. Argument, description and narrative presented effectively and appropriately. Vocabulary showing awareness of ambiguities and shades of meaning. Figurative language, such as metaphor, to convey meaning. ### Use of writing Presents analysis of argument and situation. Sustains organization of ideas, which are justified with detail in extended writing.	

Suggested new indicators

Speaking and listening
Writing
Reading

A B C D E F G H I

H Is aware of subtleties in language.
Develops analytical arguments.
Uses precise description in writing.
Edits to sharpen message.

I Writes in many genres.
Masters the craft of writing.
Is capable of powerful writing.

Contexts for observation: Curriculum focus

Writing to and with students

At this stage of development, students who demonstrate control over the necessary skills and strategies, are usually in Grade 7 or 8. This means they will usually have different teachers for Language Arts and the content areas.

Sean Walmsley (State University of NY at Albany), on commenting on the NY State English Language Arts Assessments, writes:

> All the tests combine reading and writing, but writing is the major form of assessing reading. Writing plays a much greater role in the tests than before. Writing will need to occupy a far greater portion of the language arts curriculum.

So that writing takes place across the curriculum, teachers of all subject areas could have students keep notebooks — writers notebooks, learning logs or self-reflective journals, reading-response journals and research journals for use in content areas are some examples.

These will all serve as sources for ideas or 'seeds' for drafting during the writing workshop.

Other ways that students can collect ideas and form intentions can include:

- using stream of consciousness or 'fast writing'
- recording written conversations, or dialogue journals
- collecting ideas and adding them to a list in their writing folders
- bundling — using index cards to collect and sort and order facts and ideas.

Writing with students

Writing workshop

Flexibility is essential when considering grouping arrangements. Assessment of writing and students' needs will be considered. Individuals, pairs, small-group and class-group arrangements are all part of the daily management of the writing workshop.

Teachers may be reading to the class from the work of well-known writers to model lead writing, bringing a small group to work on revision by resequencing, teaching others punctuation skills, and conducting individual conferences all in a 40–45 minute workshop.

Donald Graves (*A Fresh Look at Writing*, Heinemann, 1996) says that the conditions that the teacher establish, as well as sensitive teaching, can assist students to become 'remarkable writers'.

Speaking and listening
Writing
Reading

A B C D E F G H I

He includes the following conditions.

- *Time.* Each day drafting, revising and publishing, including handwriting, spelling and language skills, should be in the workshop.
- *Choice.* Students choose their own topics (often within a given form) when they write.
- *Response.* The response of others, in conferences, with partners and at sharing time, is critical.
- *Demonstration.* Teachers and parents need to 'think aloud' and write to and with students to continually show them how the process works.
- *Expectation.* Teachers show how and expect students to continually work to be better writers *all* in a highly structured, predictable supportive environment.

Writing by students

The New Standards and English Language Arts Standards in US school systems have focused the need for a planned approach to the modeling, guiding and explicit teaching of writing so that the students are able to respond to the demands of the standards.

Students in Sixth and Seventh Grades and beyond are expected to be able to demonstrate in writing that they:

- understand cause and effect
- can recognize the main idea and supporting details
- are able to summarize, and then use the notes to expand into a piece of writing
- can write clearly, so that understanding of sequence is seen
- can analyze characters either from their reading or in their own writing
- are able to take a stance and defend it in their writing, using several sources
- can compare and contrast
- can write to explain
- can write to teach others how to do or make something
- can write to retell, and recount.

Editing, proofreading and correcting for publishing

Students should ultimately be able to independently revise during and after drafting and composing. This will include reorganizing and restructuring words, phrases, clauses and paragraphs to make the meaning clear to their readers, and make their writing as coherent as possible.

They should be able to proofread to correct spelling, punctuation and grammar.

The following may provide both teachers and students with the processes and routines necessary for students to develop independent proofreading skills:

- word resources available to the writer — word walls (including high-frequency and topic words), writers' word books, and prefix, suffix and homophone lists on the class walls
- teaching approaches that focus on teaching, developing and using strategies, such as the 'have-a-go' process
- writing dictionaries, thesauruses, computer word-finders and spell-checkers
- teachers modeling their own spelling strategies
- the teaching, by modeling, of proofreading skills
- partner and group proofreading
- mini-lessons, specifically to teach spelling, punctuation and grammar where needed
- finding new, unusual and intriguing words while reading and adding them to personal word lists
- teachers using planned investigations of particular spelling patterns
- teachers creating a spelling awareness by assisting students to reach a wider audience for their writing, and publishing regularly.

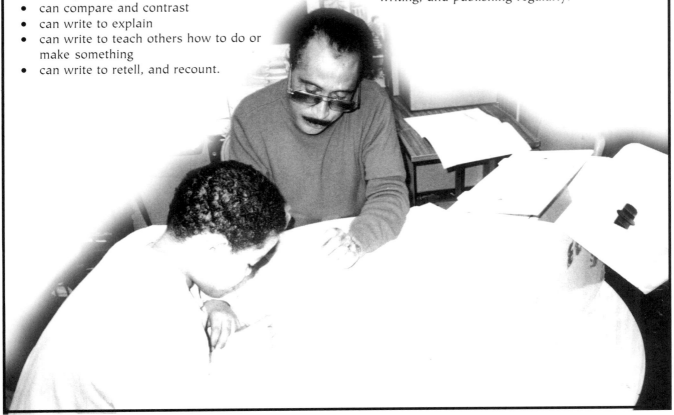

Writing profile record

Speaking and listening

Writing

Reading

A B C D E F G H I

Writing band G

Comment

What the writer does
Writes in narrative, expository and argumentative styles. Uses a range of writing styles effectively and appropriately for purpose, situation and audience. Uses a range of vocabulary effectively and appropriately for purpose, situation and audience. Edits work to improve the smooth flow of ideas and reorganizes work to make it more readable. Replaces words and sentences during revision of written work. Changes sequence of ideas, adds new ideas during revision.

What the writing shows
Main and supporting ideas presented clearly. Correct format for letters, invitations. Figurative language, such as simile, for descriptive purposes.

Use of writing
Shows a range of styles — written conversations, poems, plays, journals. Writes formal and social letters and distinguishes between the purposes of each. Adapts writing to demands of task. Completes complex forms that seek detailed biographical and related information.

Writing band H

Comment

What the writer does
Edits and revises own work to enhance effect of vocabulary, text organization and layout. Edits and revises others' writing, improving presentation and structure without losing meaning or message.

What the writing shows
Meaning expressed precisely. Organization and layout of written text accurate and appropriate for purpose, situation and audience. Argument, description and narrative presented effectively and appropriately. Vocabulary showing awareness of ambiguities and shades of meaning. Figurative language, such as metaphor, to convey meaning.

Use of writing
Presents analysis of argument and situation. Sustains organization of ideas, which are justified with detail in extended writing.

Writing band I

Comment

What the writer does
Writes with ease on most familiar topics in both short passages and extended writing. Uses analogies and symbolism in writing. Uses irony in writing. Uses figures of speech, metaphor and simile to illustrate and support message embedded in extended text. Structures a convincing argument in writing. Can use sustained and elaborated metaphorical language in writing.

What the writing shows
Extension beyond conventions of standard written English in a skillful and effective way.

Use of writing
Conveys extended arguments through writing. Adapts to demands of academic writing.

Suggested new indicators

Chapter 7

Speaking and listening profile records

Understands social conventions of spoken language and responds appropriately.
Listens attentively, interacts with the speaker and responds with interest.

Speaking and listening

Writing

Reading

A B C D E F G H I

Contexts for observation: Curriculum focus

- *Talking* with and *listening* to students during classroom activities provides the teacher with useful information about their understanding and use of oral language, demonstrated by their ideas, confidence, cooperation and responses.
- *Dramatic play* in the classroom (dress-up or costume corner) and the playground provides students with opportunities for spontaneous talk, either alone or in role play with others. They may be observed exploring concepts and enjoying language.
- *Listening to stories, songs and poems* read and told provides students with opportunities to demonstrate their growing language repertoire and understanding of sounds, rhythm, and vocabulary, and language structures of English in spoken and written form.

- Students' ability to convey and respond to information in either small or large groups during *share time* is demonstrated.
- *Dramatization* of familiar stories provides opportunities to observe students' growing confidence and ability to communicate to a large group.
- During *morning meeting time* students can share personal news in social groups. Vary the size and composition of the groups from time to time, to give them the opportunity to experience talk with different people.
- During *read aloud* and *shared reading*, students will be able to interact at appropriate times.
- *Sharing time*, following both reading and writing workshops, gives students opportunities to express their thoughts and opinions.

School .... Class ....

Name .... Term ....

	Comment
Speaking and listening band A **Uses of language** Joins in familiar songs, poems and chants. Allows others to speak without unnecessary interruption. Waits for appropriate turn to speak. Offers personal opinion in discussion. Speaks fluently to the class. Follows instructions, directions and explanations. Listens attentively to stories, songs and poems. Reacts to stories, songs and poems heard in class (smiles and comments). Recognises sounds in the environment. Begins to recall details. Begins to sequence. Follows directions during classroom routines. **Features of language** Connects phrases and clauses with 'and', 'and then', 'but'. Speaks at a rate that enables others to follow. Speaks at a volume appropriate to the situation. Hears sounds and does actions simultaneously in action songs. Hears rhyming words.	
Speaking and listening band B **Uses of language** Makes short announcements clearly. Tells personal anecdotes in discussion. Retells a story heard in class, preserving the sequence of events. Accurately conveys a verbal message to another person. Responds with facial expressions. Responds with talk when others initiate conversation. Initiates conversation with peers. Holds conversation with familiar adults. Asks what unfamiliar words mean. Uses talk to clarify ideas or experience. Listens and sustains attention for increasing periods. Talks about mental pictures after listening to stories, poems etc. Identifies meaning from speaker's voice (anger, surprise). Selects and gives options in listening activities. **Features of language** Reacts to absurd word-substitution. Demonstrates an appreciation of wit. Reacts to unusual features of language such as rhythm, alliteration or onomatopoeia. Hears initial and final sounds in words	**Comment**

Suggested new indicators

Speaking and listening

Writing

Reading

A B C D E F G H I

SPEAKING and LISTENING band

Experiments and uses language in a variety of ways. Uses talk to clarify ideas and experiences. Uses body language to assist in conveying understanding.

Listens for a range of purposes, discriminates sounds in words, and can recall stories told.

Contexts for observation: Curriculum focus

- When students engage in *informal talk* (in developmental play activities), they provide opportunities to observe them exploring language and interacting socially as they initiate and respond to talk.
- Students' experimentation with language and the creation of their own rhymes, riddles and songs provide opportunities to witness their growing vocabulary and concept development, their emotional response to texts and their awareness of the use of language to entertain.
- By listening to stories, songs and poems in the listening area (listening post, quiet-reading area), students demonstrate their recall of storylines, story and language structures, words and phrases, and share taped stories, songs and poems.

- Student responses to literature during *shared reading activities* and *retelling* provide information on their growing understanding of stories, characters, plots, settings and language structures.
- *Storytelling* and discussion provide opportunities to observe students' expression of ideas and perspectives relating to personal experiences.
- *Reading and writing conferences* allow students to demonstrate competence in communicating ideas, clarity in expressing thoughts and ability to request information and accept suggestions.
- Students demonstrate their ability to convey and respond to information in either small or large groups during *share time*.

School .... Class ....

Name.. Term ....

	Comment

Speaking and listening band A
Uses of language
Joins in familiar songs, poems and chants. Allows others to speak without unnecessary interruption. Waits for appropriate turn to speak. Offers personal opinion in discussion. Speaks fluently to the class. Follows instructions, directions and explanations. Listens attentively to stories, songs and poems. Reacts to stories, songs and poems heard in class (smiles and comments). Recognises sounds in the environment. Begins to recall details. Begins to sequence. Follows directions during classroom routines.
Features of language
Connects phrases and clauses with 'and', 'and then', 'but'. Speaks at a rate that enables others to follow. Speaks at a volume appropriate to the situation. Hears sounds and does actions simultaneously in action songs. Hears rhyming words.

Speaking and listening band B
Uses of language
Makes short announcements clearly. Tells personal anecdotes in discussion. Retells a story heard in class, preserving the sequence of events. Accurately conveys a verbal message to another person. Responds with facial expressions. Responds with talk when others initiate conversation. Initiates conversation with peers. Holds conversation with familiar adults. Asks what unfamiliar words mean. Uses talk to clarify ideas or experience. Listens and sustains attention for increasing periods. Talks about mental pictures after listening to stories, poems etc. Identifies meaning from speaker's voice (anger, surprise). Selects and gives options in listening activities.
Features of language
Reacts to absurd word-substitution. Demonstrates an appreciation of wit. Reacts to unusual features of language such as rhythm, alliteration or onomatopoeia. Hears initial and final sounds in words.

Speaking and listening band C
Uses of language
Makes verbal commentary during play or other activities with concrete objects. Speaks confidently in formal situations (assembly, report to class). Explains ideas clearly in discussion. Discusses information heard (e.g. dialogue, news items, report). Based on consideration of what has already been said, offers personal opinions. Asks for repetition, restatement or general explanation to clarify meaning. Is aware of non-verbal communication. Is learning to listen critically for main idea and supporting details. Awareness of the need to be silent, to wait and respond as appropriate. Ability to distinguish between types of speech (a chat, a warning, a joke). Listens to plan, compare and begin to make judgments.
Features of language
Sequences a presentation in logical order. Gives instructions in a concise and understandable manner. Reads aloud with expression, showing awareness of rhythm and tone. Modulates voice for effect. Nods, looks at speaker when others initiate talk. Hears middle sounds in words.

Suggested new indicators

**Is developing confidence with spoken language.
Is sensitive to voice control in specific situations.
Is developing confidence through active listening,
responding, and clarifying when meaning is not
clear.**

Contexts for observation: Curriculum focus

- Students may be observed exploring and learning about language as they *converse informally* in the playground and during practical activities. Their increasing confidence can be oberved and the clarity of their ideas and opinions in discussion.

- In *cooperative group activities* students are engaged in the varied purposes of solving problems, exploring ideas, planning and understanding practical tasks. They question, listen, clarify and support the ideas of others.

- Students' involvement in *dramatization* of familiar stories demonstrates their growing confidence and ability to communicate to a large group.

- Students' *retelling* of familiar stories enables teachers to observe them expressing and exploring their understanding of texts and language with other students.

- *Shared and choral reading* can be used to identify students' use of voice to show enjoyment and expression of the rhythm and rhyme of language.

- In *writing*, students demonstrate their ability to communicate and negotiate ideas, clarify meanings and express their thoughts.

- During *share time*, students may be observed as they report on and discuss interests, experiences, information or directions relating to something they have created.

- When students *provide instructions* to a group for playing a game or completing a classroom activity, they can be observed presenting information with confidence, using language appropriate to the audience and providing clear and concise information.

- In *share and compare conference groups*, students talk about their work with each other. This is valuable talk, where students can test their own understandings against those of their peers, taking into account the views of others as they explore a given topic.

- Give students classroom responsibilities where *talk is part of the task.* Have them greet and introduce classroom visitors and explain what is happening in the classroom. Invite others in the school community to visit and share an activity. Students may take verbal messages to others. Set up ways they can organize and delegate group responsibilities. They may take responsibility for maintaining lists, checking tasks and collecting information.

- Productive talk between students while they are engaged in literacy activities should be encouraged.

Speaking and listening

Reading   Writing

A B C D E F G H I

School .... Class ....

Name .... Term ....

Speaking and listening band B

Comment

Uses of language
Makes short announcements clearly. Tells personal anecdotes in discussion. Retells a story heard in class, preserving the sequence of events. Accurately conveys a verbal message to another person. Responds with facial expressions. Responds with talk when others initiate conversation. Initiates conversation with peers. Holds conversation with familiar adults. Asks what unfamiliar words mean. Uses talk to clarify ideas or experience. Listens and sustains attention for increasing periods. Talks about mental pictures after listening to stories, poems etc. Identifies meaning from speaker's voice (anger, surprise). Selects and gives options in listening activities.

Features of language
Reacts to absurd word-substitution. Demonstrates an appreciation of wit. Reacts to unusual features of language such as rhythm, alliteration or onomatopoeia. Hears initial and final sounds in words.

Speaking and listening band C

Comment

Uses of language
Makes verbal commentary during play or other activities with concrete objects. Speaks confidently in formal situations (assembly, report to class). Explains ideas clearly in discussion. Discusses information heard (e.g. dialogue, news items, report). Based on consideration of what has already been said, offers personal opinions. Asks for repetition, restatement or general explanation to clarify meaning. Is aware of non-verbal communication. Is learning to listen critically for main idea and supporting details. Awareness of the need to be silent, to wait and respond as appropriate. Ability to distinguish between types of speech (a chat, a warning, a joke). Listens to plan, compare and begin to make judgments.

Features of language
Sequences a presentation in logical order. Gives instructions in a concise and understandable manner. Reads aloud with expression, showing awareness of rhythm and tone. Modulates voice for effect. Nods, looks at speaker when others initiate talk. Hears middle sounds in words.

Speaking and listening band D

Comment

Uses of language
Tells personal anecdotes, illustrating in a relevant way the issue being discussed. Recounts a story or repeats a song spontaneously. Retells scenes from a film or drama. Offers predictions about what will come next. Recites poems. Asks questions in conversation. Has a second try at something to make it more precise. Arouses and maintains an audience interest during formal presentations (e.g. report to class, announcement). Hears the difference between social interactions and information transaction.

Features of language
Uses a range of vocabulary related to a particular topic. Maintains receptive body stance in conversation. Speaks in a way that conveys feelings (while keeping emotions under control). Hears consonants, vowels, blends and digraphs. Hears the difference between hard and soft vowels. Ability to listen to and recognise and give an explanation (e.g. in science). Asks for repetition or an explanation when meaning is unclear. Is able to listen to make judgments, summarize and evaluate.

Suggested new indicators

Speaking and listening

Writing

Reading

A B C D E F G H I

SPEAKING and LISTENING band D

Can recount and retell, recite with feeling, and use a range of vocabulary to arouse and maintain audience interest.

Distinguishes between social and informational listening; will seek clarification.

Speaking and listening

Writing

Reading

A B C D E F G H I

Contexts for observation: Curriculum focus

- Elicit information about students' oral language development through careful questioning and interaction during *teaching and learning* activities. Students' understanding will be demonstrated during their predicting, retelling and reporting.
- After *listening to* or *reading* stories, poems, plays or reports, or *viewing* visual performances, students' retelling provides evidence of their ability to infer, predict, select and organize information, their sense of text forms and their attitudes to language.
- *Guided reading* reveals much about students' predictive skills and their use of a range of vocabulary.
- During *shared reading* of *poetry*, students demonstrate their understanding of mood and imagery, and their emotional response to text and rhythmic expression.

- *Reader's theater* enables observation of students' use of voice to convey ideas and feelings, while arousing and maintaining audience interest.

Assessment information

Students may be taught to assess their own performance and use what they find to inform their future learning directions. The discussion can be made specific by addressing key questions such as the work requirement, the status of the work, the difference between the goal and the status of the work, and the learning improvement plan.

Help students understand how to assess by giving help when it's needed, providing opportunities to practice, modeling exactly what has to be done and said, and deciding what other issues need to be considered.

Speaking and listening profile record

	Comment
Speaking and listening band C	

Uses of language

Makes verbal commentary during play or other activities with concrete objects. Speaks confidently in formal situations (assembly, report to class). Explains ideas clearly in discussion. Discusses information heard (e.g. dialogue, news items, report). Based on consideration of what has already been said, offers personal opinions. Asks for repetition, restatement or general explanation to clarify meaning. Is aware of non-verbal communication. Is learning to listen critically for main idea and supporting details. Awareness of the need to be silent, to wait and respond as appropriate. Ability to distinguish between types of speech (a chat, a warning, a joke). Listens to plan, compare and begin to make judgments.

Features of language

Sequences a presentation in logical order. Gives instructions in a concise and understandable manner. Reads aloud with expression, showing awareness of rhythm and tone. Modulates voice for effect. Nods, looks at speaker when others initiate talk. Hears middle sounds in words.

Speaking and listening band D	Comment

Uses of language

Tells personal anecdotes, illustrating in a relevant way the issue being discussed. Recounts a story or repeats a song spontaneously. Retells scenes from a film or drama. Offers predictions about what will come next. Recites poems. Asks questions in conversation. Has a second try at something to make it more precise. Arouses and maintains an audience interest during formal presentations (e.g. report to class, announcement). Hears the difference between social interactions and information transaction.

Features of language

Uses a range of vocabulary related to a particular topic. Maintains receptive body stance in conversation. Speaks in a way that conveys feelings (while keeping emotions under control). Hears consonants, vowels, blends and digraphs. Hears the difference between hard and soft vowels. Ability to listen to and recognise and give an explanation (e.g. in science). Asks for repetition or an explanation when meaning is unclear. Is able to listen to make judgments, summarize and evaluate.

Speaking and listening band E	Comment

Uses of language

Presents a point of view to a large audience. Presents materials with consideration for audience needs. Speculates and puts forward a tentative proposition. Uses logic, arguments or appeals to feelings to persuade others. Explores concepts related to concrete materials by describing, narrating or explaining how things work and why things happen. Dramatizes familiar stories, showing understanding. Uses convincing dialogue to role-play short scenes involving familiar situations or emotions. Invites others to participate. Takes initiative in raising new aspects of an issue. Asks questions to elicit more from an individual. Answers questions confidently and clearly in interviews. Asks for the meaning of familiar words used in unfamiliar ways. Listens to compare and find relationships in stories, poems, and conversations. Listens to analyze and hypothesize.

Features of language

Makes links between ideas in discussions. Uses complex connectives in speech, such as 'although', 'in spite of', 'so that'. Uses syntactical structures — principal and subordinate clauses. Uses vocabulary appropriate to audience and purpose. Distinguishes between words of similar meaning. Identifies the sounds of vowels, consonants, digraphs and blends. Uses awareness of sounds to identify consonants and vowels. Uses sounds to identify prefixes, suffixes, compounds and syllables.

Suggested new indicators	

Speaking and listening

Writing

Reading

A B C **D** E F G H I

SPEAKING and LISTENING band

Uses logic, argument and questioning to clarify ideas and understanding appropriate to audience and purpose. Accepts others' opinions and is developing listening strategies — listening for relationships in stories, poems, etc.

Contexts for observation: Curriculum focus

- *Cooperative group activities* provide opportunities to observe students as they take on roles that help communication in the group and the achievement of group goals.
- In all areas of the curriculum, groups of students will be observed as they *question, discuss and debate* issues that arise from their investigations. In presenting their findings to a larger group, students will demonstrate their increased precision and control of the use of language.
- During *cooperative cloze activities*, students will be involved in critical exploration of text, language structures and the author's ideas. They speculate, consider the contribution of others and negotiate various points of view.
- *Guided reading* provides students with opportunities to demonstrate understanding of character, plot and points of view, and ability to infer meanings that underlie texts.
- *Brainstorming* and *concept mapping* in modeled and shared writing involve students in discussion of a topic where they can verbalise the links and connections they make with their own knowledge and experiences.
- Make opportunities to *engage children in talk* — greet them when they come into class, chat with them while they work and start conversations in the school grounds and outside school in the community.

- How students are grouped for *work sessions* can also be varied. There are many ways of grouping and each one has advantages for talk. These may include:
  - *heterogeneous groups* — mixed-sex, single-sex, friendship and cross-age
  - *homogenous groups* — interests, skill-learning needs and specific needs
  - *cooperative groups and jigsaw groups* — in group 1, individuals plan what they think and will say; in group 2, individuals take a partner to 'pair and share'; in group 3, three pairs meet as a larger group to 'norm and storm' a consensus view to present to the whole group.
- A *wall chart* can also be made for assessing talks (see below).

A good listener:	A good speaker:
• faces the speaker	• faces the listener/s
• responds with the whole body, keeping it still to listen, nodding and shaking head in response to the speaker	• knows what he or she wants to say, thinks about it, thinks about the listener and plans to match what is said with this listener
• waits for the right pause to reply	
• paraphrases the speaker's ideas and information to affirm meaning	• varies the voice to say it better
• asks well-focused questions	• checks that the listener understands before going further
• uses gestures to support and add further information	• asks well-focused questions
• maintains constant eye contact	• uses gestures to support and add further information
• pauses for the speaker to respond	• maintains constant eye contact
• gives sufficient opportunities for the speaker to respond.	• pauses for the listener to respond
	• gives sufficient opportunities for the listener to respond.

School .... Class ....

Name .... Term ....

Speaking and listening band D

Comment

Uses of language
Tells personal anecdotes, illustrating in a relevant way the issue being discussed. Recounts a story or repeats a song spontaneously. Retells scenes from a film or drama. Offers predictions about what will come next. Recites poems. Asks questions in conversation. Has a second try at something to make it more precise. Arouses and maintains an audience interest during formal presentations (e.g. report to class, announcement). Hears the difference between social interactions and information transaction.

Features of language
Uses a range of vocabulary related to a particular topic. Maintains receptive body stance in conversation. Speaks in a way that conveys feelings (while keeping emotions under control). Hears consonants, vowels, blends and digraphs. Hears the difference between hard and soft vowels. Ability to listen to and recognise and give an explanation (e.g. in science). Asks for repetition or an explanation when meaning is unclear. Is able to listen to make judgments, summarize and evaluate.

Speaking and listening band E

Comment

Uses of language
Presents a point of view to a large audience. Presents materials with consideration for audience needs. Speculates and puts forward a tentative proposition. Uses logic, arguments or appeals to feelings to persuade others. Explores concepts related to concrete materials by describing, narrating or explaining how things work and why things happen. Dramatizes familiar stories, showing understanding. Uses convincing dialogue to role-play short scenes involving familiar situations or emotions. Invites others to participate. Takes initiative in raising new aspects of an issue. Asks questions to elicit more from an individual. Answers questions confidently and clearly in interviews. Asks for the meaning of familiar words used in unfamiliar ways. Listens to compare and find relationships in stories, poems, and conversations. Listens to analyze and hypothesize.

Features of language
Makes links between ideas in discussions. Uses complex connectives in speech, such as 'although', 'in spite of', 'so that'. Uses syntactical structures — principal and subordinate clauses. Uses vocabulary appropriate to audience and purpose. Distinguishes between words of similar meaning. Identifies the sounds of vowels, consonants, digraphs and blends. Uses awareness of sounds to identify consonants and vowels. Uses sounds to identify prefixes, suffixes, compounds and syllables.

Speaking and listening band F

Comment

Uses of language
Asks speaker to clarify ambiguities. Asks questions to draw information from the group. Indicates disagreement in a constructive manner. Attempts to resolve disagreement or misunderstanding. Supports constructively the statements of others. Attempts to keep discussion on the topic. Makes formal introductions with courtesy and clarity. Tells a story with expression and emphasis, showing confidence, highlighting key points and demonstrating the storyteller's art. Explores abstract ideas (justice, good and evil) by generalizing, hypothesizing or inferring. Uses thinking skills in listening activities to hypothesize.

Features of language
Uses a range of idiomatic expressions with confidence. Reacts to an inappropriate choice of words. Makes positive interjections. Distinguishes intensity, pitch, quality and sequence of a variety of sounds.

Suggested new indicators

Speaking and listening

Reading Writing

A B C D E F G H I

SPEAKING and LISTENING band

F

Can persuade and influence peers, using language. Clarifies and orders thoughts in conversation. Expresses ideas, feelings, opinions, and can generalize or hypothesize. Can infer meanings when appropriate. Links stories and spoken forms of language to values. Is aware of relevance and irrelevance, pitch intensity, and intonation.

Contexts for observation: Curriculum focus

- Engagement in *informal debating activities* provides students with opportunities to demonstrate their ability to contribute positively to the functioning of the group as they argue, debate and negotiate alternative points of view.
- Students' discussion and comparison of their predictions and confirmative evidence in *guided reading* provide insights into their understanding of vocabulary, a range of issues and text forms.
- Students' ability to facilitate group processes will be demonstrated by their active listening and participation in *small-group discussion* as they restate, question and clarify information to achieve the group's goal.
- Exploration of issues and topics through *critical analysis* of visual and written text provides evidence of students' analysis and synthesis of information.
- Students' *use of voice, gesture and personality* to convey and express feelings, images, mood and experience is evidence of their command of and confidence in using language, understanding of issues and awareness of audience needs.
- Exploration of conflict situations through *role play* provides insights into students' ability to resolve constructively disagreements and misunderstandings.
- *Formal introductions* and responses to guests and visiting speakers provide students with opportunities to display confidence in speaking to a large group and a command of language to fulfill social conventions.
- *Prediction* before and during shared and guided reading allows students to discuss and compare and confirm, using evidence. This provides insights into their understanding of vocabulary, a range of issues and text forms.
- Set aside a day, perhaps each term, for *author's day*, when children can read from their writing and discuss with others what they have written. Arrange for the following:
  - a special chair that is the author's chair
  - a chairperson who is responsible for introducing each author and providing biographical information for the audience
  - an invitation to parents and other class groups and teachers to attend.
- Roster students to collect information about the day's upcoming events and news and present it as a *daily news bulletin* to the class.

- As the most experienced and adept speaker and listener in the classroom, it is up to the teacher to model the *conventions of social talk* — how it looks and sounds — and to demonstrate to students the behaviors expected by it:
  - how to take turns
  - how to listen
  - how to plan ideas and information first and then to express these clearly
  - how to respond to others.

Good teachers value time spent talking with students, and respond to their conversation in the same way as they share talk and respond to other adults-with courtesy, care and attention. Students learn social talk from such interactions.

School .... Class ....

Name .... Term ....

Speaking and listening profile record

Speaking and listening band E **Uses of language** Presents a point of view to a large audience. Presents materials with consideration for audience needs. Speculates and puts forward a tentative proposition. Uses logic, arguments or appeals to feelings to persuade others. Explores concepts related to concrete materials by describing, narrating or explaining how things work and why things happen. Dramatizes familiar stories, showing understanding. Uses convincing dialogue to role-play short scenes involving familiar situations or emotions. Invites others to participate. Takes initiative in raising new aspects of an issue. Asks questions to elicit more from an individual. Answers questions confidently and clearly in interviews. Asks for the meaning of familiar words used in unfamiliar ways. Listens to compare and find relationships in stories, poems, and conversations. Listens to analyze and hypothesize. **Features of language** Makes links between ideas in discussions. Uses complex connectives in speech, such as 'although', 'in spite of', 'so that'. Uses syntactical structures — principal and subordinate clauses. Uses vocabulary appropriate to audience and purpose. Distinguishes between words of similar meaning. Identifies the sounds of vowels, consonants, digraphs and blends. Uses awareness of sounds to identify consonants and vowels. Uses sounds to identify prefixes, suffixes, compounds and syllables.	**Comment**
Speaking and listening band F **Uses of language** Asks speaker to clarify ambiguities. Asks questions to draw information from the group. Indicates disagreement in a constructive manner. Attempts to resolve disagreement or misunderstanding. Supports constructively the statements of others. Attempts to keep discussion on the topic. Makes formal introductions with courtesy and clarity. Tells a story with expression and emphasis, showing confidence, highlighting key points and demonstrating the storyteller's art. Explores abstract ideas (justice, good and evil) by generalizing, hypothesizing or inferring. Uses thinking skills in listening activities to hypothesize. **Features of language** Uses a range of idiomatic expressions with confidence. Reacts to an inappropriate choice of words. Makes positive interjections. Distinguishes intensity, pitch, quality and sequence of a variety of sounds.	**Comment**
Speaking and listening band G **Uses of language** Asks interview questions that are relevant. Extends another group member's contribution by elaboration or illustration. Helps others to put forward ideas. Summarizes the conclusions reached in a group discussion. Takes initiative in moving discussion to the next stage. Reflects and evaluates discussion (e.g. What have we learned? How did we do it?). Dramatizes scenes from complex stories, showing understanding of dramatic structure. Uses appropriate introductions and conclusions according to purpose and context. Identifies and uses different strategies for responding to listener feedback. Responds to audience by adjusting features such as pace, tone or volume, to sustain interest. **Features of language** Varies tone, pitch, pace of speech to create effect and aid communication. Self-corrects a poor choice of words. Talks or writes about special forms of language, such as accents or dialects. Identifies and discusses the typical structures and features of poems, songs, fables, advertisements, speeches and commentaries.	**Comment**

Suggested new indicators

SPEAKING and LISTENING band G

Uses language increasingly to explore ideas, question, and summarize discussions.
Uses tone to create effect and to aid communication.
Explores and reflects on ideas while listening.
Is becoming familiar with a range of spoken forms of language and is able to distinguish between them for purpose, meaning, and appropriate audience.

Contexts for observation: Curriculum focus

- Through summarizing, restating, clarifying and elaborating in *cooperative groups*, students demonstrate their positive and active involvement in discussion.
- The collection of information from teachers, parents and other students through surveys and *interviews* provides students with opportunities to demonstrate their ability to use a variety of questioning techniques, to select and organize relevant information and to listen and respond appropriately to the ideas of others.
- *Critical analysis* of scripted text reveals students' awareness of the particular features of oral and written language.
- *Peer* and *cross-age tutoring* provides information about a student's ability to present information clearly using appropriate language, content and supportive listening strategies to encourage a partner's participation.
- Rehearsal and interpretation of a scene from a play

in *drama workshop* provide opportunities to observe students' articulation and defence of interpretation, as well as their organization and expression of ideas through voice and action.
- *Improvisation* in role play provides evidence of students' understanding of issues, inference from text, and use of dialogue and gesture to express interpretations and points of view.
- *Exploration* of speech functions and different spoken text types is important. Students must experience how to select appropriate vocabulary and how to incorporate introductions and conclusions, and structures such as comparison and contrast. They learn to respond to punctuation and text features such as italic and bold text.
- *Formative assessment* happens when students are provided with feedback on their presentations and encouraged to make informed comments about others' performances based on agreed criteria.

School .... Class ....

Name .... Term ....

Speaking and listening

Speaking and listening band F

Uses of language
Asks speaker to clarify ambiguities. Asks questions to draw information from the group. Indicates disagreement in a constructive manner. Attempts to resolve disagreement or misunderstanding. Supports constructively the statements of others. Attempts to keep discussion on the topic. Makes formal introductions with courtesy and clarity. Tells a story with expression and emphasis, showing confidence, highlighting key points and demonstrating the storyteller's art. Explores abstract ideas (justice, good and evil) by generalizing, hypothesizing or inferring. Uses thinking skills in listening activities to hypothesize.

Features of language
Uses a range of idiomatic expressions with confidence. Reacts to an inappropriate choice of words. Makes positive interjections. Distinguishes intensity, pitch, quality and sequence of a variety of sounds.

Comment

Speaking and listening band G

Uses of language
Asks interview questions that are relevant. Extends another group member's contribution by elaboration or illustration. Helps others to put forward ideas. Summarizes the conclusions reached in a group discussion. Takes initiative in moving discussion to the next stage. Reflects and evaluates discussion (e.g. What have we learned? How did we do it?). Dramatizes scenes from complex stories, showing understanding of dramatic structure. Uses appropriate introductions and conclusions according to purpose and context. Identifies and uses different strategies for responding to listener feedback. Responds to audience by adjusting features such as pace, tone or volume, to sustain interest.

Features of language
Varies tone, pitch, pace of speech to create effect and aid communication. Self-corrects a poor choice of words. Talks or writes about special forms of language, such as accents or dialects. Identifies and discusses the typical structures and features of poems, songs, fables, advertisements, speeches and commentaries.

Comment

Speaking and listening band H

Uses of language
Experiments with and reflects on possible readings and interpretations of a piece of scripted drama. Sustains cogent arguments in formal presentation. Holds conversation with less familiar adults (e.g. guest speaker). Contributes to group discussions, Is able to give considered reasons for own opinions. Gives prepared talks presenting some challenging themes and issues. Is able to use technology such as an overhead projector or data-show projector to enhance communication. Is able to find implied or stated meanings after listening to persuasive speeches. Listens to spoken texts with challenging themes and issues and is able to summarize the main issues.

Features of language
Defines or explains words to cater for audience needs. Comments on bias or point of view in spoken language. Analyzes factors that contribute to the success or otherwise of discussion. Identifies how linguistic features, such as emotive language, humor and anecdotes, can be used to engage audiences.

Comment

Suggested new indicators

Reading   Writing

A B C D E F **G** H I

SPEAKING and LISTENING band

Uses and appreciates nuances of language to affect an audience. Monitors and modifies communication to aid understanding. Distinguishes emotive rhetoric from reasoned argument. Analyzes spoken genres for meaning and underlying messages.

Speaking and listening

Writing

Reading

A B C D E F G H I

Contexts for observation: Curriculum focus

- Active participation in *cooperative group discussion* is demonstrated by students' summarizing of discussion, restatement of group goals, elaboration of the ideas of others and questioning to assist the participation of other group members.
- During focused *critical analysis* of visual narratives and reports, students will demonstrate their understanding of varied use of verbal and visual images to persuade or influence an audience.
- Students demonstrate personal characterization and interpretation through their use of dialogue, gesture and action in video presentations, theater and drama workshops.
- Development of scripts for *dramatization* of an issue or text provides evidence of students' understanding and use of dialogue and dialectic devices to inform, entertain and persuade.
- *Formal reports*, *debates* and *expert panel presentations* demonstrate students' abilities to inform or persuade

through organizing and presenting issues and ideas to a variety of audiences.
- *Influence on audience* techniques may be studied. Students may experiment with techniques such as use of vocabulary, rhythm, intonation, timing, pausing, body language and facial expression.
- In classroom contexts that involve *listening for specific purposes*, students can learn strategies to listen to the spoken texts of others and to identify strategies used to influence a particular audience. Guided listening experiences may alert them to how tone, pitch and pace of speech affect presentation. The need to learn about discourse markers, such as 'in summary . . . ' or 'let me stress this point . . . ', are used by speakers to indicate a change of topic or an important point.

	Comment
Speaking and listening band G **Uses of language** Asks interview questions that are relevant. Extends another group member's contribution by elaboration or illustration. Helps others to put forward ideas. Summarizes the conclusions reached in a group discussion. Takes initiative in moving discussion to the next stage. Reflects and evaluates discussion (e.g. What have we learned? How did we do it?). Dramatizes scenes from complex stories, showing understanding of dramatic structure. Uses appropriate introductions and conclusions according to purpose and context. Identifies and uses different strategies for responding to listener feedback. Responds to audience by adjusting features such as pace, tone or volume, to sustain interest. **Features of language** Varies tone, pitch, pace of speech to create effect and aid communication. Self-corrects a poor choice of words. Talks or writes about special forms of language, such as accents or dialects. Identifies and discusses the typical structures and features of poems, songs, fables, advertisements, speeches and commentaries.	
Speaking and listening band H **Uses of language** Experiments with and reflects on possible readings and interpretations of a piece of scripted drama. Sustains cogent arguments in formal presentation. Holds conversation with less familiar adults (e.g. guest speaker). Contributes to group discussions, Is able to give considered reasons for own opinions. Gives prepared talks presenting some challenging themes and issues. Is able to use technology such as an overhead projector or data-show projector to enhance communication. Is able to find implied or stated meanings after listening to persuasive speeches. Listens to spoken texts with challenging themes and issues and is able to summarize the main issues. **Features of language** Defines or explains words to cater for audience needs. Comments on bias or point of view in spoken language. Analyzes factors that contribute to the success or otherwise of discussion. Identifies how linguistic features, such as emotive language, humor and anecdotes, can be used to engage audiences.	
Speaking and listening band I **Uses of language** Makes effective use of visual or other materials to illustrate ideas. Capitalizes on opportunities offered by responses to interview questions. Asks interview questions designed to elicit extended responses. Participates effectively in debates, meetings and other structured situations characterised by complexity of purpose, procedure and subject matter. Combines improvised and prepared text to engage and entertain audience. Listens to a range of spoken texts, such as radio or television interviews, before taking part in critical discussion. Thinks about sociocultural background, age and knowledge of speaker in panel or interviews in order to frame appropriate questions. **Features of language** Talks or writes about subtle effects of dialogue between characters in film or drama. Uses puns and double meanings. Comments on tone, attitude or emphasis in speech. Talks about quality of speech, such as loudness, pitch, pronunciation, articulation and dialect. Stresses key words to ensure audience attentiveness and understanding. Uses pauses to emphasize important points. Selects aspects of written research assignment for presentation in speech, making necessary adjustments to style and content. Controls pitch, timing, sequencing of content and style of delivery to maximize the impact of spoken texts presenting complex themes or issues. Listens to and builds on the ideas of others. Listens to and challenges the ideas of others through questions, asking for clarification. Evaluates elements of persuasion and appeal in spoken texts. Is able to identify the subtle ways in which spoken language can be used to manipulate an audience. Is able to adopt appropriate language conventions in formal speech settings.	
Suggested new indicators	

Speaking and listening

Reading   Writing

A B C D E F G H I

SPEAKING and LISTENING band

Uses language proficiently in its many forms.
Is able to evaluate and respond to content and points of view.
Is a skilled listener, able to distinguish emotive and persuasive rhetoric and to analyze a wide range of spoken genres while listening.

Contexts for observation: Curriculum focus

- When *reporting* on the outcomes of an investigation, students demonstrate their ability to use maps, diagrams, models, extracts and audiovisual aids to help structure and illustrate the information presented.
- After watching visual text (theater, film and television), *critical analysis* of elements of the performance allows students to demonstrate their understanding of how these elements contribute to the effect of the performance on an audience.
- Students plan and develop *formal arguments* about complex issues and learn to use evidence systematically to justify points of view and to develop logical conclusions.

- Students study an increasing range of *linguistic features* such as rhetorical devices and their emotional appeal to the listener, and learn to identify and use discourse markers which signal to the listener how a text is structured. These activities also allow them to investigate the language use of effective communicators.
- To enhance their *formal presentations*, students select from a range of strategies such as using audio and visual equipment to record their presentation and check timing, using technology such as overhead and data-show projectors, organizing a room to maximize audience impact, or judging audience engagement and adjusting pace or deleting text as appropriate.

School .... Class ....
Name.. Term ....

Speaking and listening band H

Uses of language

Experiments with and reflects on possible readings and interpretations of a piece of scripted drama. Sustains cogent arguments in formal presentation. Holds conversation with less familiar adults (e.g. guest speaker). Contributes to group discussions, Is able to give considered reasons for own opinions. Gives prepared talks presenting some challenging themes and issues. Is able to use technology such as an over-head projector or data-show projector to enhance communication. Is able to find implied or stated meanings after listening to persuasive speeches. Listens to spoken texts with challenging themes and issues and is able to summarize the main issues.

Features of language

Defines or explains words to cater for audience needs. Comments on bias or point of view in spoken language. Analyzes factors that contribute to the success or otherwise of discussion. Identifies how linguistic features, such as emotive language, humor and anecdotes, can be used to engage audiences.

Comment

Speaking and listening band I

Uses of language

Makes effective use of visual or other materials to illustrate ideas. Capitalizes on opportunities offered by responses to interview questions. Asks interview questions designed to elicit extended responses. Participates effectively in debates, meetings and other structured situations characterised by complexity of purpose, procedure and subject matter. Combines improvised and prepared text to engage and entertain audience. Listens to a range of spoken texts, such as radio or television interviews, before taking part in critical discussion. Thinks about sociocultural background, age and knowledge of speaker in panel or interviews in order to frame appropriate questions.

Features of language

Talks or writes about subtle effects of dialogue between characters in film or drama. Uses puns and double meanings. Comments on tone, attitude or emphasis in speech. Talks about quality of speech, such as loudness, pitch, pronunciation, articulation and dialect. Stresses key words to ensure audience attentiveness and understanding. Uses pauses to emphasize important points. Selects aspects of written research assignment for presentation in speech, making necessary adjustments to style and content. Controls pitch, timing, sequencing of content and style of delivery to maximize the impact of spoken texts presenting complex themes or issues. Listens to and builds on the ideas of others. Listens to and challenges the ideas of others through questions, asking for clarification. Evaluates elements of persuasion and appeal in spoken texts. Is able to identify the subtle ways in which spoken language can be used to manipulate an audience. Is able to adopt appropriate language conventions in formal speech settings.

Comment

Suggested new indicators

Speaking and listening

Reading   Writing

A B C D E F G H I

Section 3
Reporting with profiles

Chapter 8

Recording and reporting with profiles

Using the scale to record an assessment

Recording and reporting information about learning has been a difficult issue for many teachers, buildings and districts. There has been a huge amount of research into assessment issues, but very little into reporting and next to none into recording methods. Portfolios have been developed in recent years as a means of storing assessment information, but the communication of assessments has remained unchanged from grade levels, per cent scores or grades. There is little available to give teachers and parents — and others with an interest in student growth and development — about three pieces of information that are important for planning, evaluation and resource allocation.

- What can the students do?
- What rate of progress are they making?
- How do they compare with their peers and with established standards?

The reporting and recording mechanisms developed in concert with the profiles help to answer these questions and to present information to constituencies ranging from students, parents and teachers to administrators, district officials and the general public.

Reporting and recording assessments with the profiles will be illustrated with an example of a student who has been developing in reading and writing a little more slowly than his peers. His name is Gary.

Gary is a Sixth Grade 6 boy. He is 14 years old. Obviously, he is older than is usual for his grade level. Progress has not been automatic. Teachers had been encouraging him to write on a range of topics for some years without a great deal of success; then, in Fifth Grade, his teacher discovered Gary's passion for racing cars and allowed him to read and write and prepare his class talks on this topic without restriction. Gary suddenly became interested in writing, and 'read' as many car magazines as he could lay his hands on; he now willingly seeks out stories and writes on this topic. He was watching the San Marino Grand Prix when Ayrton Senna crashed. His story of the event follows.

The rating scale

The first method of illustrating and keeping records of an assessment is a rating scale. It is a simple exercise for the teacher to develop overall views of student progress; it is also used for large-scale assessment and survey work when a building or a district or even a state wishes to gather data on a large number of students. Chapter 10 shows this data clearly and discusses the measurement properties of the data and of teacher judgment used to carry out the assessments.

In the first part, a simple rating scale is used to illustrate the application of the profiles in developing a

numerical form of reporting and recording the assessment. More on the assessments is presented in chapter 9, dealing with a reading classroom, and then more are illustrated in the section dealing with large-scale assessment.

It is not difficult to assess Gary's writing. It is not usually appropriate to assess from a single piece of writing; normally, we would expect many more pieces to be used and a portfolio of writing samples to form the basis of the assessment. However, in this case we are providing just one piece to illustrate how simple it is to place a student on the scales. Given the background information above and a small amount of writing (approximately the fifth draft of text), we are able to gauge Gary's level. In the following example, we can see that Gary has progressively shown indicators of writing development. Starting from band A, the comment section shows how he was rated using the profile and a simple rating scale to record the extent to which he exhibited the indicators at each level.

Gary's writing is rated using 3, 2 or 1 for each band level. A 3 means that we believe he is beyond that level, a 2 means that he is developing at that level, a 1 means 'beginning' and a 0 means that we believe that he has not yet reached that level.

It is possible to present different forms of reports that illustrate answers to the following questions.
- Where is Gary now?
- What has his rate of progress been?
- How does he compare with his peers — at the building, the district and other levels in the system (norms)?

Writing band A

What the writer does
Uses writing implement to make marks on paper. Explains the meaning of marks (word, sentence, writing, letter). Copies 'words' from signs in immediate environment. 'Reads', understands and explains own 'writing'.

What the writing shows
Understanding of the difference between picture and print. Use of some recognizable symbols found in writing.

Use of writing
Comments on signs and other symbols in immediate environment. Uses a mixture of drawings and 'writing' to convey and support an idea.

Comment 3
- Gary certainly makes marks, copies words from the environment, even the newspaper.
- We can conclude that Gary is beyond band A.

Writing band B

What the writer does
Reproduces words from signs and other sources in immediate environment. Holds pencil/pen using satisfactory grip. Uses preferred hand consistently for writing. Attempts to put 'words' in 'sentence' format. 'Writes' a simple message. Uses sound–symbol linkages. 'Captions' or 'labels' drawings.

What the writing shows
Use of vocabulary of print (letters, words, question marks, etc.). Use of letters of the alphabet and other conventional symbols. Use of letters in groups to form words. Placing of spaces between groups of 'letters'. Knowledge that writing moves from left to right in lines from top to bottom of page.

Use of writing
Writes own name.

Interests and attitudes
Understands that writing is talk written down.

Comment 3
- He is reproducing words from the newspaper and other media.
- He uses all of these conventions.
- Words, spaces, directionality.
- Signs his name at the end of the work.

Writing band C

What the writer does
Commences writing without assistance. Has a personalized handwriting style that meets most handwriting needs. Checks written work by reading it aloud. Sounds out words as an aid to spelling.

What the writing shows
Legible writing with recognizable words. Words put together in sentence format. Words written in a logical order to make a sentence that can be read. Upper and lower case letters used conventionally. Written sentences that can be understood by an adult.

Use of writing
Sentences convey message on one topic. Uses 'I' in writing. Writes about feelings, judgment or direct experience. Creates characters from experience and immediate environment.

Comment 3
- Gary will write on racing cars without prompting, uses sentences and has paragraph structure.
- Writing is legible, upper and lower case are used and the text can be read by an adult.
- He writes in the first person, expresses feelings and creates characters from his environment.

Writing band D

What the writer does
Marks most common words with incorrect spelling when editing writing. Uses ideas, themes and structure from books in writing. Uses concepts of order and time in writing. Reads, rereads and revises own written work. Uses everyday words in appropriate written context.

What the writing shows
Punctuation used conventionally. Conventional spelling used most of the time; spelling showing recall of visual patterns. Stories that can be read, understood and retold by classmates. Several sentences constructed on one topic in a logical order. A smooth connection of ideas. Beginning, middle and end in narrative writing.

Use of writing
Writes stories containing characters from outside personal environment. Writes with ease on most matters of personal experience. Writes on a variety of topics. Writes personal anecdotes and letters to friends. Writes for a known audience. Uses a range of written forms — poems, letters, journals, logs, etc.

Comment 2
- Can edit his work (this is the fifth version of his text), revises writing.
- Punctuation is not used conventionally. story could be read by classmates with difficulty.
- Sentences vary in logical sequence, order of ideas is established.
- Does not write on a range of topics, but is restricted.
- In most aspects Gary has not yet moved beyond band D.

Writing band E

What the writer does
Edits work to a point where others can read it; corrects common spelling errors, punctuation and grammatical errors. Develops ideas into paragraphs. Uses a dictionary, thesaurus or word-checker to extend and check vocabulary for writing. Uses vivid, specific language.

What the writing shows
Sentences with ideas that flow. Paragraphs with a cohesive structure. Ability to present relationships and to argue or persuade. Messages in expository and argumentative writing identifiable by others, although some information may be omitted. Brief passages written with clear meaning, accuracy of spelling and apt punctuation. Appropriate shifts from first to third person in writing. Consistent use of the correct tense. Appropriate vocabulary for familiar audiences such as peers, younger children or adults, with only occasional inappropriate word choice. Compound sentences, using conjunctions. Variations of letters, print styles or fonts. A print style appropriate to task and a consistent handwriting style.

Use of writing
Writes a properly sequenced text that has a convincing setting. Creates characters from imagination.

Comment 1
- Common spelling errors are not all corrected, the writing still contains punctuation and grammatical errors.
- Gary is only showing very early signs of band E behaviour, if any at all.

Writing band F

What the writer does
Writes sentences in different forms: statement, question, command, explanation. Writes paragraphs to develop logical sequence of ideas. Corrects most spelling, punctuation and grammatical errors in editing others' written work. Consults available sources to improve or enhance writing. Joins letters, using linkages where appropriate, to form personal handwriting style.

What the writing shows
Narratives containing introduction, complication and resolution in a logical order. Longer descriptions and narratives developed coherently. Use of both active and passive voice. A range of vocabulary and grammatical structures. Complex sentences — principal and subordinate clauses. Higher level writing skills in areas of special interest. Understanding of the difference between narrative and other forms of writing.

Use of writing
Completes standard forms requiring personal information. Makes appropriate use of narrative and other forms of writing.

Comment 0
- Lacks capacity to write in different forms.
- Coherence of narrative depends on a sympthetic reader.
- Lacks complex sentences.
- Shows no understanding of different forms of writing in this piece.
- Gary has not yet reached band F.

Writing band G

What the writer does

Writes in narrative, expository and argumentative styles. Uses a range of writing styles effectively and appropriately for purpose, situation and audience. Uses a range of vocabulary effectively and appropriately for purpose, situation and audience. Edits work to improve the smooth flow of ideas and reorganizes work to make it more readable. Replaces words and sentences during revision of written work. Changes sequence of ideas, adds new ideas during revision.

What the writing shows

Main and supporting ideas presented clearly. Correct format for letters, invitations. Figurative language, such as simile, for descriptive purposes.

Use of writing

Shows a range of styles — written conversations, poems, plays, journals. Writes formal and social letters and distinguishes between the purposes of each. Adapts writing to demands of task. Completes complex forms that seek detailed biographical and related information.

The literacy rocket

It is possible to develop a graphic representation of a student's progress using the nutshell statements and a graph illustrating the full range of the continuum. If the range where a student group is expected to be developing is located on the graph (from the descriptive data in chapter 10) and the teacher then adds each student's approximate level of development, a very rich contextualised description of student performance becomes available. This is illustrated in Figure 8.1, which we call the *literacy rocket*. There are several components to the rocket. First, the nutshell statements illustrate the progression of literacy described by the profiles. Second, the box in the stem of the rocket presents the expected level for the middle 50 per cent of a year-level cohort. Finally, the rocket presents the teacher with an opportunity to place a student on the profile scale using both normative and criterion-referenced information. Note that since the nutshell statements can be translated into several languages, parents who do not speak English can be *shown in graphic* form, their child's progress in literacy.

This is such a simple task. Suppose that Gary's work was contained in a portfolio with reading logs, tapes of his speaking, reports of his discussions and so on; the teacher would only need to build the profile once every few weeks. The richness of the assessment would feed into teaching and be based directly on the assessment of the student's work. The teacher only has to mark the rocket as illustrated with a small shaded region to show Gary's progress; now Gary and his parents can be shown what he has achieved, where he is heading, and how he compares with others in Sixth Grade. We have here both norm-referenced interpretation and criterion-referenced interpretation on the same report. Blackline masters of the rocket are provided in appendix III for all profile scales.

Recording rate of progress

Another form of individual record keeping and reporting was devised by a school district in New York State; they adapted box plots and whisker plots and made them fit their own school. Box and whisker plots are a graphic way of presenting the distribution of student performance (see Chapter 10); they present the standards of the school (or any other descriptive data) and allow the student growth to be monitored from year to year and compared with those data. The report is accompanied with the full text of the profiles. Obviously, the use of criterion-referenced reporting and recording formats allows great flexibility and enormous communication ability on the part of the teacher and the school. Gary's progress can now be plotted over a number of years; the teacher can plot his level on the profiles at the same time each year, perhaps in the spring, and illustrate how he has grown and developed. The norm (box) for the grade level can be used as a reference point and used to illustrate the rate of progress. In Gary's case, there has been dramatic growth in both reading and writing from Fifth Grade to Sixth Grade; if this information is supplemented with portfolio examples of his work, parents and teachers alike can gain a very clear understanding of his development. This is illustrated in Figure 8.2, in which his level is represented by the dot (●) under the box plots. His progress over the six years of school is represented by his position in the spring term each year, when his achievement with regard to reading, writing and spoken language on the profiles has been plotted and the information added to his portfolio.

The permanent record of Gary's language arts development shows some remarkable development in the upper elementary years. Teachers would see that Gary has had a slow beginning and the teacher who recorded such a dramatic jump in development would almost certainly be asked what had happened. What was the evidence for such a change? This clearly overcomes an important difficulty in assessment programs — labeling; students can often be labeled as underachievers and given little encouragement to improve. Gary's teacher, however, can show that improvement is occurring, and so the potential for Gary to be labeled as a permanent underachiever is diminished. Moreover, because it is a decision and a judgment made on the basis of continuous information and observation in class, there is little chance that the change will be dismissed as an

Writing profile rocket

I — Writes in many genres. Masters the craft of writing. Is capable of powerful writing.

Is aware of subtleties in language. Develops analytical arguments. Uses precise descriptions in writing. Edits to sharpen message. — **H**

G — Uses rich vocabulary, and writing style depends on topic, purpose and audience. Produces lively and colorful writing. Can do major revisions of writing.

Can describe things well. Can skillfully write and tell a story or describe phenomena. Now has skills to improve writing. — **F**

E — Can plan, organize and polish writing. Writes in paragraphs. Uses vocabulary and grammar suited to topic. Can write convincing stories.

Can write own stories. Changes words and spelling until satisfied with the result. — **D**

C — Now says something in own writing. Is writing own sentences. Is taking interest in appearance of writing.

Is learning about handwriting. Knows what letters and words are and can talk about ideas in own writing. Is starting to write recognizable letters and words. — **B**

A — Knows that writing says something. Is curious about environmental print. Is starting to see patterns.

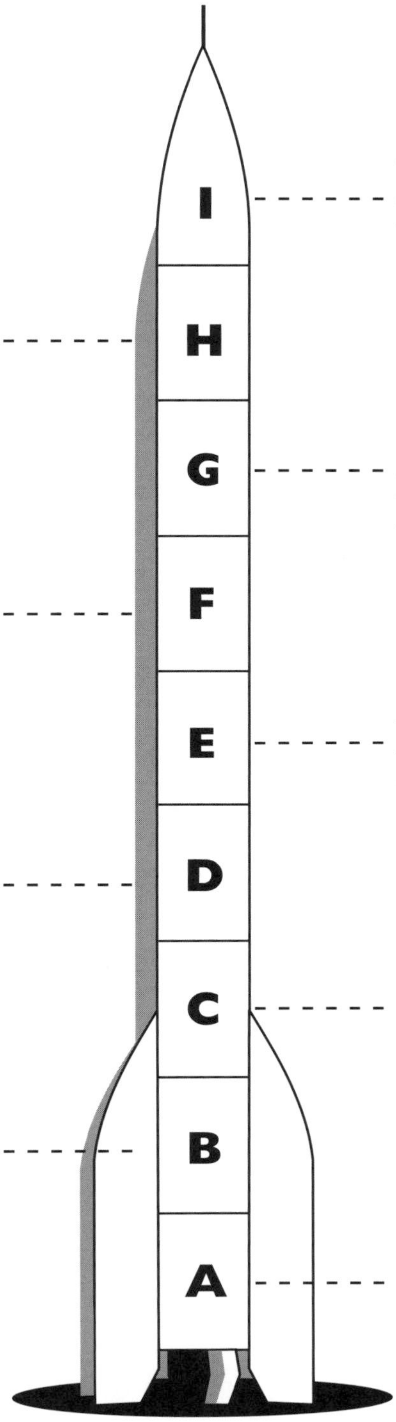

50% of the Sixth Grade students can be located within this range. Norms for all grades can be identified by locating the 'box' from the box and whisker plot in Chapter 10 for the relevant skill.

The student is estimated to be at about this location on the profile. See the worked example from writing shown on pages 98–100.

Figure 8.1

aberration attributable to a different testing program or to coaching for a testing program. The profiles can, as in the case of Gary, help to overcome many of the negative aspects of assessment.

In this case, the teachers in the school collected the data and developed the school's own box and whisker plots for the report. It is also possible to use norms from the research studies on profiles. For this reason, blackline masters based on average expected rates of progress — as demonstrated by a sample of over 2000 students — have been presented in the appendix for school use. Schools could perhaps develop their own norms over a number of years and use a stab set of box plots; in the meantime, it is suggested that the plots presented in the appendix are used.

The class record

Using a standard class list, the profiles can be mapped onto the list using the nutshell statements to illustrate levels of growth. This helps to establish local comparisons and to give the teacher a continuous overview of the relative development of all students in the class.

The class record forms included in appendix III can be copied and covered with a laminating sheet or with plastic so that a water-based felt pen can be used to show growth, adding a different color each term. A thermometer approach (that is, adding small bits to the record as improvement is seen and matched to the bands) would be best in this case so that the development and accumulation of skills can be seen. Examples of Gary's class are illustrated in Figure 8.3. It can be seen that some students have made more progress than others, but Gary's progress is shown to be spectacular and recent.

In this example it can be seen that although Gary is below the expected range for his grade level, there are other students in the class who are at similar levels. The range in the class is quite large and the teacher needs to develop an instructional approach to compensate for the range of development; this alone illustrates to teachers and others that one approach alone can never work successfully. Graphic reports may be supplemented with descriptive reports, but generally teachers will not have time to write long descriptive reports about student development; instead, profiles provide the opportunity to use the indicators to frame descriptive reports that show what the students have completed, what they are working on now and the next signs of progress that can be expected. Parents also can be involved in helping to develop those signs by working with the students. The descriptive report on page 105 describes Gary's progress; this style of report might be best accompanied by the box plot style overview or by the rocket chart in order to put the report into context.

Central School District

Student .Gary. . . . .

It is important to note that the reading and writing bands do not interrelate; therefore, no comparison should be made between the two.

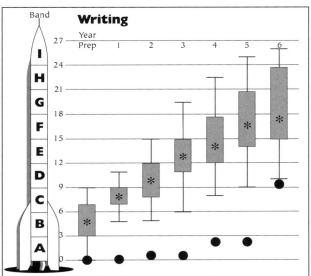

Reading

Teacher comment

Gary's reading has improved this year as he has had the opportunity to develop his interest in car racing literature. He is reading many magazines and newspaper articles on the topic and has found an area of reading that may have many other relevant themes in future.

Writing

Teacher comment

Gary's writing has also improved as he has taken the opportunity to write on his favorite theme. His difficulties with skin problems have not impeded his progress this year. He is also beginning to write letters and other forms of writing related to his topic of car racing. Gary is clearly the most knowledgable person in the school on this topic and his writing reflects his expertise.

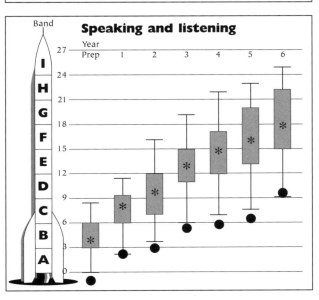

Speaking and listening

Teacher comment

Gary's use of media language on the topic of cars is noticeable. He has developed his vocabulary this year by extending his observations into themes related to the central theme of cars. He has successfully participated in a television program for schools and helped prepare the class for this activity. His spoken language skills have developed well under this type of activity.

Figure 8.2

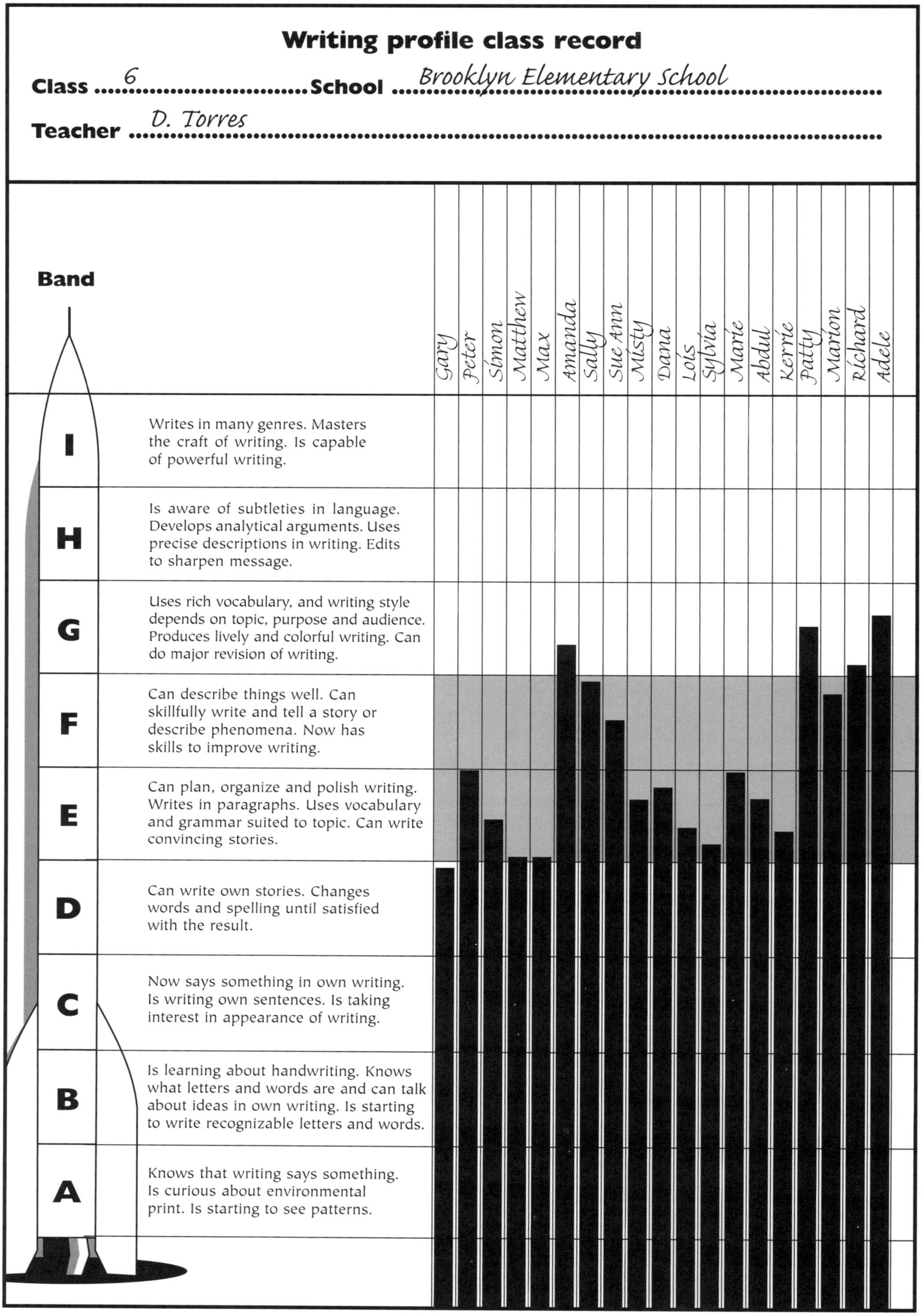

Writing profile class record

Class ....6............... School ....Brooklyn Elementary School........

Teacher ....D. Torres..

Band

Students (columns): Gary, Peter, Simon, Matthew, Max, Amanda, Sally, Sue Ann, Misty, Dana, Lois, Sylvia, Marie, Abdul, Kerrie, Patty, Marion, Richard, Adele

Band	Description
I	Writes in many genres. Masters the craft of writing. Is capable of powerful writing.
H	Is aware of subtleties in language. Develops analytical arguments. Uses precise descriptions in writing. Edits to sharpen message.
G	Uses rich vocabulary, and writing style depends on topic, purpose and audience. Produces lively and colorful writing. Can do major revision of writing.
F	Can describe things well. Can skillfully write and tell a story or describe phenomena. Now has skills to improve writing.
E	Can plan, organize and polish writing. Writes in paragraphs. Uses vocabulary and grammar suited to topic. Can write convincing stories.
D	Can write own stories. Changes words and spelling until satisfied with the result.
C	Now says something in own writing. Is writing own sentences. Is taking interest in appearance of writing.
B	Is learning about handwriting. Knows what letters and words are and can talk about ideas in own writing. Is starting to write recognizable letters and words.
A	Knows that writing says something. Is curious about environmental print. Is starting to see patterns.

Figure 8.3

Gary is reading a wider range of materials now. He is able to identify appropriate reading materials for his interests and tends to read a lot of materials on racing cars if the materials are well illustrated and the captions are simple. He is prepared to tackle some materials on cars even when the text is difficult. This is particularly true if there are many pictures to help with the reading. He will need to broaden his reading materials in the next year. He seeks out classmates and others in the school to discuss the materials he reads.

His written work also reflects the books he reads. He writes his own stories and can check his spelling to a limited degree. His grammar will soon improve as he learns more about sentences and paragraphs and as he reads a wider range of materials. He writes about the things he has seen on TV and in the newspapers about car racing. The writing also reflects the conversations he holds with his classmates and others at school. His range of topics is limited but recently he has begun to write letters and other forms of writing. He can be expected to improve in both range and content of writing in the near future as he begins to develop ways of planning his writing and his command of grammar and spelling.

Chapter 9

The reading classroom

Assessment as a natural part of teaching and learning

Classrooms are busy places where in the course of daily activities — the culture of the classroom, the interactions of the learners with others in the classroom, the production of oral and written texts, the teacher's and children's understanding of the learning process, and the classroom setting itself — all have a part to play. The reading classroom described in some detail in this section — a Fifth–Sixth Grade — is no exception; however, the structure and information-gathering processes could be typical of other grade levels, and this will be demonstrated.

In this group, students chose books from the class library, the school library and their personal libraries both for silent reading time and for reading at home because of the teacher's belief that the opportunity to read self-selected materials silently should occur every day. Silent reading, demonstrated by role models such as the teacher, the principal and parents, was vital to show the students that reading was valued. The actual daily timetabling of silent reading reinforced its importance and provided time for reading that might not otherwise have happened in busy lives. The students kept reading logs, which provided evidence of the numbers and kinds of books read. These texts were discussed in groups, and sometimes with the teacher. The teacher also chose books to read to the students: books that enabled them to develop strategies — or ways of thinking about texts — in order to see them as meaningful and to take pleasure in how and what their reading made them think.

The students were readers who had already learned how to use the semantic, syntactic and graphophonic cueing systems described in a sociopsycholinguistic approach to reading. The school was very supportive of the profile approach to assessment and had adopted it in its school policy. The teachers liked the fact that the profile scale was developed to enable them to focus on achievements and outcomes in learning in a way that allowed for the idiosyncrasies of individual students as they developed their reading skills.

The literacy profiles had been chosen because the school administration realized that their use would overcome some of the difficulties inherent — as they saw the situation — in reading tests and comprehension tests per se. There were seen to be important differences between reading as it occurs in tests and reading as it occurs in everyday life. Reading-test passages are usually much shorter than those in everyday texts, and the cognitive processing used to integrate a shorter text is different and less elaborate than that used in a longer one. Also, a good reader is someone who can resist the emotional appeals of a text by understanding how it works. Reading passages used in tests tend to be matter of fact, emotionally neutral, and able to be handled objectively. The literacy profiles allowed for the collection of data about the students' reading when the teaching and learning was taking place. The indicators of development accumulated in an observable fashion as the students' reading abilities progressively emerged and their knowledge of the reading process expanded.

John: a pen picture

The following example shows, in more detail, how the teacher used the literacy scale to synthesize information from broad descriptions of the reading and learning behavior of a ten-year-old student, John. Initially the teacher began to form a picture of John's reading strategies and habits from work samples, reading lists and end-of-year descriptive reports from his previous teacher and his parents. This information would be very unwieldy but for the indicators on the scale, which provide a manageable way of rating progress. The indicators are evidently present in the student's work and they provide a common vocabulary for describing progress.

John had come into the class with a report that described him as 'not very interested and unwilling to work consistently'. (Unhelpful descriptions like this were quite usual reading before the profiles provided common criteria for teachers to focus on in discussion.) He liked reading information books in silent reading time, but had a history of being distracted and of annoying others when he was supposed to be listening to a story. His handwriting was poorly formed, without a personal style. In his self-evaluation at the beginning of the year he wrote, 'I listen good and I talk good but when I read I sometimes get stuck on the words'. He indicated that he wasn't keen on writing because he had difficulty spelling words conventionally.

John was placed on the profile's reading scale at the beginning of the school year. The teacher used a highlighter pen to show these attributes; here the highlighted sections are indicated with shading (see page 107). This highlighting of what the student can do is more powerful than a checklist, which seems to emphasise what the student has yet to learn.

Although John represents the students at the lower end of the scale in this class, he does have basic reading strategies.

John's profile shows that he has established most of the behaviors described in reading band C. He is able to use all the strategies needed as a reader to seek meaning. In fact, he is showing many strategies indicated in reading band D. He is able to identify the main

Reading band C	**Comment**

Reading strategies

Rereads a paragraph or sentence to establish meaning. Uses context as a basis for predicting meaning of unfamiliar words. Reads aloud, showing understanding of purpose of punctuation marks. Uses picture cues to make appropriate responses for unknown words. Uses pictures to help read a text. Finds where another reader is up to in a reading passage.

Responses

Writing and artwork reflect understanding of text. Retells, discusses and expresses opinions on literature, and reads further. Recalls events and characters spontaneously from text.

Interests and attitudes

Seeks recommendations for books to read. Chooses more than one type of book. Chooses to read when given free choice. Concentrates on reading for lengthy periods.

Reading band D	**Comment**

Reading strategies

Reads material with a wide variety of styles and topics. Selects books to fulfill own purposes. States main idea in a passage. Substitutes words with similar meanings when reading aloud. Self-corrects, using knowledge of language structure and sound–symbol relationships. Predicts, using knowledge of language structure and/or sound/symbol to make sense of a word or a phrase.

Responses

Discusses different types of reading materials. Discusses materials read at home. Tells a variety of audiences about a book. Uses vocabulary and sentence structure from reading materials in written work as well as in conversation. Uses themes from reading in artwork. Follows written instructions.

Interests and attitudes

Recommends books to others. Reads often. Reads silently for extended periods.

idea in a passage and select books to fulfill his own purposes, although these purposes do not include reading fiction for pleasure. The profiles are formative here because they show that it is in the areas of response and attitude that there are gaps in John's reading behavior, and this points to ways in which he could be helped. He needs to learn the pleasures of reading fiction: to be turned on to story. There are some problems with self-esteem, which probably have resulted from concentration by a previous teacher on surface features such as spelling and handwriting. These demand attention.

That the profiles place assessment in a teaching and learning context is shown in the case of John by the fact that the teacher is the assessment instrument who collects information throughout the school day. The assessment program has a wash-back effect on the teaching and learning contexts: the students need to encounter literature and respond to it, so the first context is whole-class discussion of literature sessions, when the teacher reads aloud serials or shorter picture storybooks, and initiates discussion. Such sessions are used often as times to help students find appropriate ways to think about and discuss their reading. The adult or more expert peer would support the cognitive work of the student, focusing his or her attention on the main points, scaffolding toward solution. In these large-group experiences the teacher demonstrates strategies that helped understanding of the process. John needs

to learn the pleasures of reading, which include predicting, finding clues, interpreting signs and arguing about the author's intent; these are some of the ways in which readers construct texts. He needs to take risks and understand that reading starts with individual response, which is pleasurable, to refine through social construction of meaning in a group. He needs to find out that his contributions to group discussions will be valued and used in a joint construction of meaning.

Further questions broaden the picture of John's beliefs and reinforce the view that his strategic knowledge is sound.

This questioning allows the teacher to find out about

When you come to something you do not understand, what do you do?	When I come to something I have problems with, I sometimes read the sentence again and figure out what the word is.
If you knew someone was having difficulty, how would you help that person?	I'd ask them to sound the word out and keep trying. But if they can't, I'd tell them.

the students' views of what it is to be a reader. The teacher believes that there is a complex relationship between students' knowledge and thinking, and teach-

Reading profile rocket

Class .... School ....

Teacher .... Student ....*John*..

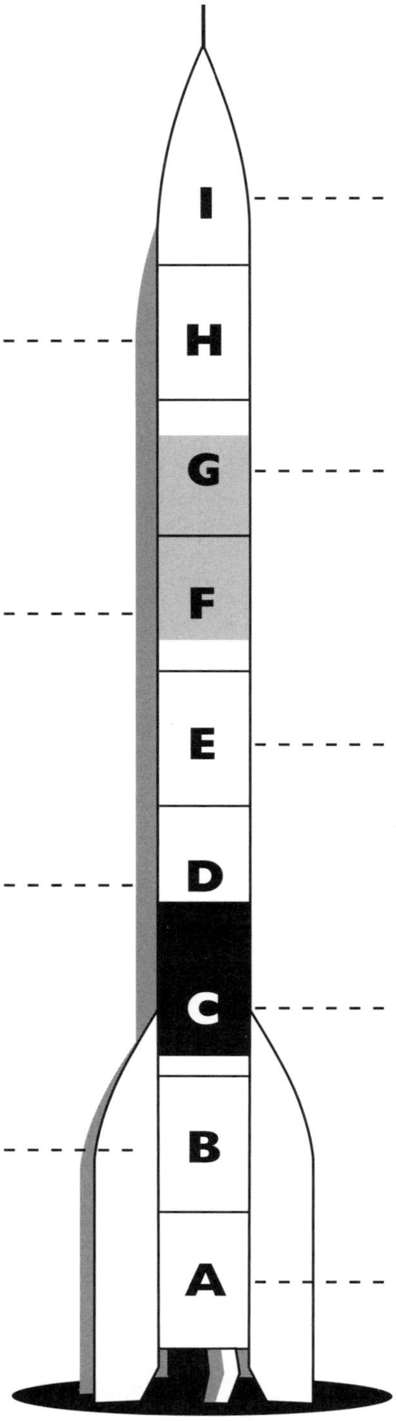

Is clear about own purpose for reading. Reads beyond literal text, and seeks deeper meaning. Can relate social implications to text.

Is familiar with a range of genres. Can interpret, analyze and explain responses to text passages.

Expects and anticipates sense and meaning in text. Discussion reflects grasp of whole meanings.
Now absorbs ideas and language.

Recognizes many familiar words. Attempts new words. Will retell story from a book. Is starting to become an active reader.
Is interested in own writing.

Is skillful in analyzing and interpreting own response to reading. Can respond to a wide range of text styles.

Reads for learning as well as pleasure. Reads widely and draws ideas and issues together.
Is developing a critical approach to analysis of ideas and writing.

Will tackle difficult texts. Writing and general knowledge reflect reading. Literacy response reflects confidence in settings and character.

Looks for meaning in text. Reading and discussion of text shows enjoyment of reading. Shares experience with others.

Knows how a book works.
Likes to have books and stories read.
Likes to talk about stories.
Displays reading-like behavior.

50% of the Sixth Grade students can be located within this range. Norms for all grades can be identified by locating the 'box' from the box and whisker plot in Chapter 10 for the relevant skill.

The student is estimated to be at about this location on the profile. See the worked example from writing shown on pages 98–100.

Figure 9.1

ing: the students' conceptions about reading — its nature, purposes and functions — are a result of interaction between their prior knowledge about reading and the reading events experienced in the classroom.

Elizabeth

A reading inventory was used to collect more data to help determine the 'starting point' of understanding. Each student in the class was surveyed concerning his or her beliefs about or attitudes to reading; for example, they were asked to indicate the particular reasons they thought someone was a good reader, and what they themselves could do to improve as readers. The following extract is from Elizabeth's written interview at the start of the year.

These answers indicate Elizabeth's concern with

| When makes her a good reader? | She is a good reader because she speaks loudly and holds her book lower than her face. |
| What would you like to do better as a reader? | I could speak louder and lower my book. |

oral reading behavior; because everyone had concentrated on getting her to raise her normally quiet voice, this aspect of reading had come to assume undue importance. She had become even more reluctant to participate in discussions.

Jason

Teachers of beginning readers should learn the attributes in the early bands and keep the first nutshell statements in mind as they help their students to become readers. Jason's teacher kept some anecdotal records of his first months at school and placed them in a portfolio for future reference.

October 16   *Jason still resists coming together with the group for storytime. He is very active and restless. He hasn't been read to at home and his mother reports that he isn't interested in reading his take-home books with her. I have had a talk to him about being good to his mother and reading her a story.*

October 18   *When we were all reading the big book* The Hungry Giant, *Jason started taking an interest when they were reading loudly, 'I'll hit you with my bommy-knocker'. He began to*

join in, too.

October 20   *Jason and Chuck had two copies of Mem Fox's* Possum Magic *and were checking to see if Hush was missing in the same picture in each book. They borrowed a copy each of Margaret Mahy's* The Lion in the Meadow. *Who wants to match rabbit's ears as a pre-reading activity. You have to learn how books work.*

November 2   *Jason and Jane were sorting and arranging the Dr Seuss books. They browsed through some and discussed the jokes, helped by the pictures. He is now one of the first to come for storytime and sits entranced. The power of story!*

December 10   *Jason's mother told me today that he never misses 'reading' with her now. She reads the book to him first. When he reads to me he is starting to talk about the letters in his name that are the starting ones for words in the book. He also recognizes a few words, e.g the, see, fish, too. He has been reading the books made in class in silent reading time, and talking about them. I wrote in his Log book that he could be encouraged to point as he was reading to get the idea of one to one.*

The teacher highlighted Jason's reading profile (see page 110).

Tanya

Tanya is in Grade 2. She had had many book experiences before starting school and learned to read very easily. This year seems to have been one of consolidation for Tanya; there are only a few new attributes on her reading profile. She has continued to be an avid reader and her log shows that she is reading denser and longer texts. There is evidence that she likes to reread books read by the teacher to the class.

The following comments are taken from transcriptions of discussions after being read stories by Anthony Browne.

April 15   *Commenting on Anthony Browne's* Willy the Wimp: *'The ending was a big surprise. I thought he had got really strong. He's a hero and then bang. But he had been a hero in a way'.*

April 18   *Commenting on Anthony Browne's* Gorilla: *'I'm catching on to Anthony Browne. People can be like animals. She wanted her father to*

Tanya's reading log

Date	Title and author	Parent's comment	Teacher's comment
April 5	*Peace at Last* by Jill Murphy	Enjoyed the humor.	Read to group.
April 16	*Possum Magic* by Mem Fox	Talked about illustrations.	Read to group.
April 17	*Oliver Button is a Sissy* by Tomie de Paola	Said, 'This is the longest book I've read'.	Read her first chapter book.

Reading band A

Jason

Comment

Concepts about print

Holds the book right way up. Turns pages from front to back. On request, indicates the beginnings and ends of sentences. Distinguishes between upper and lower case letters. Indicates the start and end of a book.

Reading strategies

Locates words, lines, spaces, letters. Refers to letters by name. Locates own name and other familiar words in a short text. Identifies known, familiar words in other contexts.

Responses

Responds to literature (smiles, claps, listens intently). Joins in familiar stories.

Interests and attitudes

Shows preference for particular books. Chooses books as a free-time activity.

Reading band B

Comment

Reading strategies

Takes risks when reading. 'Reads' books with simple, repetitive language patterns. 'Reads', understands and explains own 'writing'. Is aware that print tells a story. Uses pictures for clues to meaning of text. Asks others for help with meaning and pronunciation of words. Consistently reads familiar words and interprets symbols within a text. Predicts words. Matches known clusters of letters to clusters in unknown words. Locates own name and other familiar words in a short text. Uses knowledge of words in the environment when 'reading' and 'writing'. Uses various strategies to follow a line of print. Copies classroom print, labels, signs, etc.

Responses

Selects own books to 'read'. Describes connections among events in texts. Writes, role-plays and/or draws in response to a story or other form of writing (e.g. poem, message). Creates ending when text is left unfinished. Recounts parts of text in writing, drama or artwork. Retells, using language expressions from reading sources. Retells with approximate sequence.

Interests and attitudes

Explores a variety of books. Begins to show an interest in specific type of literature. Plays at reading books. Talks about favorite books.

be nice like the gorilla and when she got up there's a banana in his pocket to show it. In Piggybook the pigs are the father and the boys when they are bad'.

Tanya has demonstrated that familiarity with an author's works enables her to make connections that help her interpret meaning, but she hasn't yet the experience to explain these very clearly. Her enjoyment is enhanced through close looks at texts. Tanya's profile would show progress as far as band E in her responses to reading, but her strategies include those found in band D (see Tanya's Reading profile rocket on page 111).

The class group

The profiles help teaching and reporting in a way that is consistent with good teaching practice because they enhance the quality of communication in regard to achievement, attitudes, skills, strategies used and so on. These things are not easily described by any test scores, but the progress of Jason, Elizabeth, Tanya and John is easily documented from a wealth of evidence. The profiles crystallize and record the information gained by the teacher as test-instrument.

Essentially, student profiles are built by teachers simply teaching and observing the students in the classroom. No further changes need to be made to the daily routine. Teachers teach. They ask questions, set work to be done, give tests, collect work from the students, conference with the students. All the time they are gathering information about the students. Sometimes they are not even aware that they are collecting assessment information. Irregular reference to profile statements helps them to interpret information collected routinely as part of the teaching process. Sometimes the teacher needs to take time to note direct observations; the notes can include details of who is being observed and the context of observation. The following extract is part of a teacher's notes on the class.

The group were very excited and had difficulty practicing polite turn-taking in the small-group discussion. Amber barely waited for the previous speaker to finish as her thoughts raced along. Kirsten, normally very patient, joined in excitedly. They all listened with the usual respect to Max, but most unusually, John and Amber challenged his view, once again rushing to speak. They didn't convince him but they are becoming really confident that their interpretation can be just as right as Max's.

Reading profile rocket

Class .... School...

Teacher .... Student ..... *Tanya*

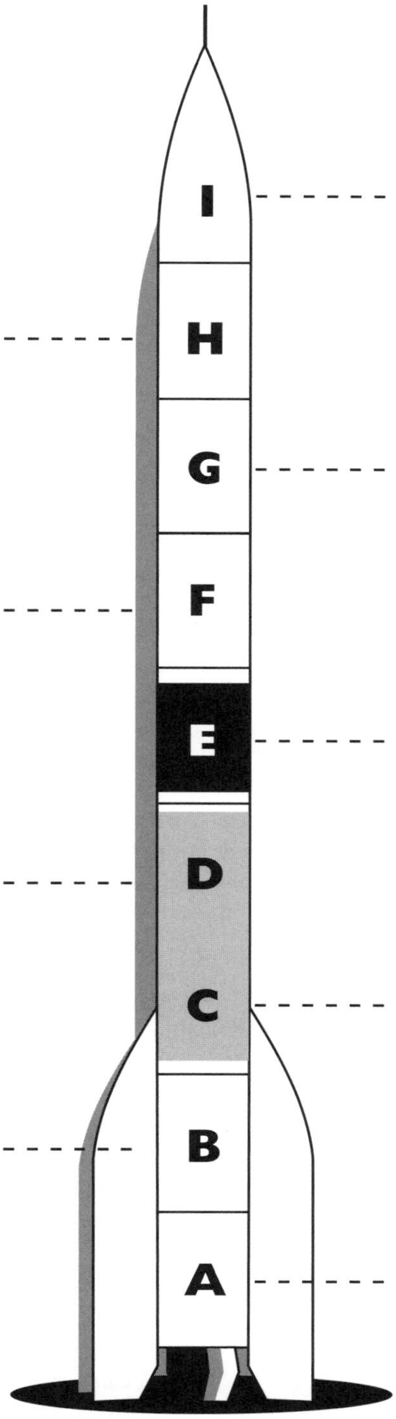

I — Is skillful in analyzing and interpreting own response to reading. Can respond to a wide range of text styles.

Is clear about own purpose for reading. Reads beyond literal text, and seeks deeper meaning. Can relate social implications to text. — H

G — Reads for learning as well as pleasure. Reads widely and draws ideas and issues together. Is developing a critical approach to analysis of ideas and writing.

Is familiar with a range of genres. Can interpret, analyze and explain responses to text passages. — F

E — Will tackle difficult texts. Writing and general knowledge reflect reading. Literacy response reflects confidence in settings and character.

Expects and anticipates sense and meaning in text. Discussion reflects grasp of whole meanings. Now absorbs ideas and language. — D

C — Looks for meaning in text. Reading and discussion of text shows enjoyment of reading. Shares experience with others.

Recognizes many familiar words. Attempts new words. Will retell story from a book. Is starting to become an active reader. Is interested in own writing. — B

A — Knows how a book works. Likes to have books and stories read. Likes to talk about stories. Displays reading-like behavior.

50% of the Second Grade students can be located within this range. Norms for all grades can be identified by locating the 'box' from the box and whisker plot in Chapter 10 for the relevant skill.

The student is estimated to be at about this location on the profile. See the worked example from writing shown on pages 98–100.

Figure 9.2

Other notes were references to circumstances or events that provided useful information. These included moods, health and personal events.

Amber told me today that they had to talk the music teacher into making a better time for concert practice. 'The other grades didn't care but we didn't want to miss Literature Groups'. It's probably fortunate that John is the music teacher's son! She is very excited about his change in attitude to reading this year.

As the volume of observation grows, it is possible for the teacher to see patterns emerging in the reading processes — sometimes individual patterns, sometimes group patterns. To briefly summarize, in the two short extracts quoted above it is possible to discover indicators of quality talk, attitude to reading, the social structure of the classroom and engagement in explaining and defending of understanding. The teacher can now refer to the profiles for pointers of group response to reading and other reading behavior that is evident when group work is used as a class activity.

The central focus is on the students as thinkers, exploring and helping each other move beyond initial understandings and their personal responses to new interpretations and broadening of world views in transactions with specific texts. Sometimes audiotapes were made of the discussions. This is well illustrated in the following extract.

Elizabeth: *The ending was funny. I suppose it meant he had to be an emu to have another big bird for a mate.*

John: *He hadn't seen an emu before so he didn't know it was the best thing to be.*

Max: *It was about the best thing to be is yourself. Be satisfied. The illustrator really made Edward look like a lion and a snake but I felt sad and embarrassed for him. It wasn't going to work, all that copying.*

John: *The snake was best.*

Kirsten: *I was thinking all the time about why doesn't some kid in the crowd call out that there's an ostrich in the monkey cage or the reptile house. That would be what would happen for real.*

Max: *In real life if you pretend you're clever or something, no one says anything. They're too polite.*

Kirsten: *I suppose the author is saying that even if you are great at pretending and it seems natural, it's still better to be yourself and things will turn out better.*

Elizabeth: *And meet another emu.*

This text showed Elizabeth taking on her usual role of initiating the discussion by introducing her puzzlement about the ending of the picture storybook and John suggesting a solution. He is joining in quite naturally now. Max continues to build on their connections, and uses his own feelings to discuss the protagonist's lack of success in finding his real self, while Kirsten

has listened and considered an anomaly — and why the author/illustrator has made this decision. Max picks up on her line of thought. Elizabeth makes a small joke — unusual for her. They have discussed the meaning of life as readers making transactions with text. They have become readers who have considered philosophical issues about perception as they make transactions with text.

Even the brief, previous discussion of the students' responses implies that the teacher is bringing legitimate, tacit knowledge to the interpretation of the situation. Because the teacher is a human instrument, she is able to bring this experiential knowledge of the students into use. John's predictions near the end of the book show him shaping his final predictions, although some wish fulfillment is still apparent rather than deep transactions with the text.

I think Trotter will come and get Gilly or Gilly's mum will come and see Gilly. Gilly might run away from her grandmother's house. Trotter and W.E. and Mr Randolph might come and live with Gilly and her grandmother.

Given information from only a small cross-section of John's reading activities, it is easy to see his progress. He now knows the excitement of tackling a difficult text. He is beginning to have confidence in predicting and talking about the setting, point of view and other ways in which the text influences the reader. He is starting to explain his responses. His teacher has by now been able to highlight all the indicators in bands C and D, and he is showing many in band E and some in band F.

All students keep what are called journals. These are portfolios of work that include some reflective writing. In an effort to get away from the view of response as 'doing an interesting activity at the end', different strategies are tried.

Students were introduced to the idea of think-alouds (an example by John is given below) as a way to show what questioning and image-making was going on in their heads as they read. These think-alouds have several advantages over other types of verbal reporting; they lessen the problem of memory failure, since the reporting is nearly concurrent with the process being described, and they are highly specific to the task and so produce reliable results. The students were asked to try these think-alouds on several occasions, but they found them tedious and so were not asked to use the technique very often. John's think-aloud gives evidence of active transactions that show how much he has now learned about the process.

I can see him in a striped prisoner suit. What an exaggeration. He's going on a bit much about being sent to a cattery. I'm into it here. The author must really be showing us what an exaggerator he is. I'm still wondering what his revenge will be. Perhaps he'll go on holiday without them. No. That's stupid. He is a cat. It'll have to be something a real cat would do normally and it will look like he's done it on purpose.

On occasion, the students were asked to write 'before' and 'after' predictions for the text. They were also asked to write their responses after a chapter had been read. These personal responses were often used in group discussion to help in the social construction of new meaning and final understanding of the text.

The following example illustrates how these kinds of data become available. Amber's response after reading shows her using personal feelings to interpret the puzzles and the metaphor of the seeds, and then come to an understanding of life cycles.

I can understand why Sam doesn't want to go back to the Red Rocks because if I had been looking after my sister and had gone away for a minute and when I got back and found she was gone, I wouldn't want to go back there. The only reason why Mum, Dad and Grandpa could go and see the marble carving by the rocks was because they didn't want Sam to think it was his fault. Life goes on even if your loved ones die. Sometimes you have just to forget about the past and concentrate on the future. The seeds that Sam blows away are a sort of sign that life goes on and new life starts.

Writing profile class record

Class ..... 6 ..... School ..... Brooklyn Elementary School .....

Teacher ..... A van Dyken .....

Band

Students: John, Stephanie, Daniel, Kirsten, Elizabeth, Angus, Amber, Max

I — Writes in many genres. Masters the craft of writing. Is capable of powerful writing.

H — Is aware of subtleties in language. Develops analytical arguments. Uses precise descriptions in writing. Edits to sharpen message.

G — Uses rich vocabulary, and writing style depends on topic, purpose and audience. Produces lively and colorful writing. Can do major revisions of writing.

F — Can describe things well. Can skillfully write and tell a story or describe phenomena. Now has skills to improve writing.

E — Can plan, organize and polish writing. Writes in paragraphs. Uses vocabulary and grammar suited to topic. Can write convincing stories.

D — Can write own stories. Changes words and spelling until satisfied with the result.

C — Now says something in own writing. Is writing own sentences. Is taking interest in appearance of writing.

B — Is learning about handwriting. Knows what letters and words are and can talk about ideas in own writing. Is starting to write recognizable letters and words.

A — Knows that writing says something. Is curious about environmental print. Is starting to see patterns.

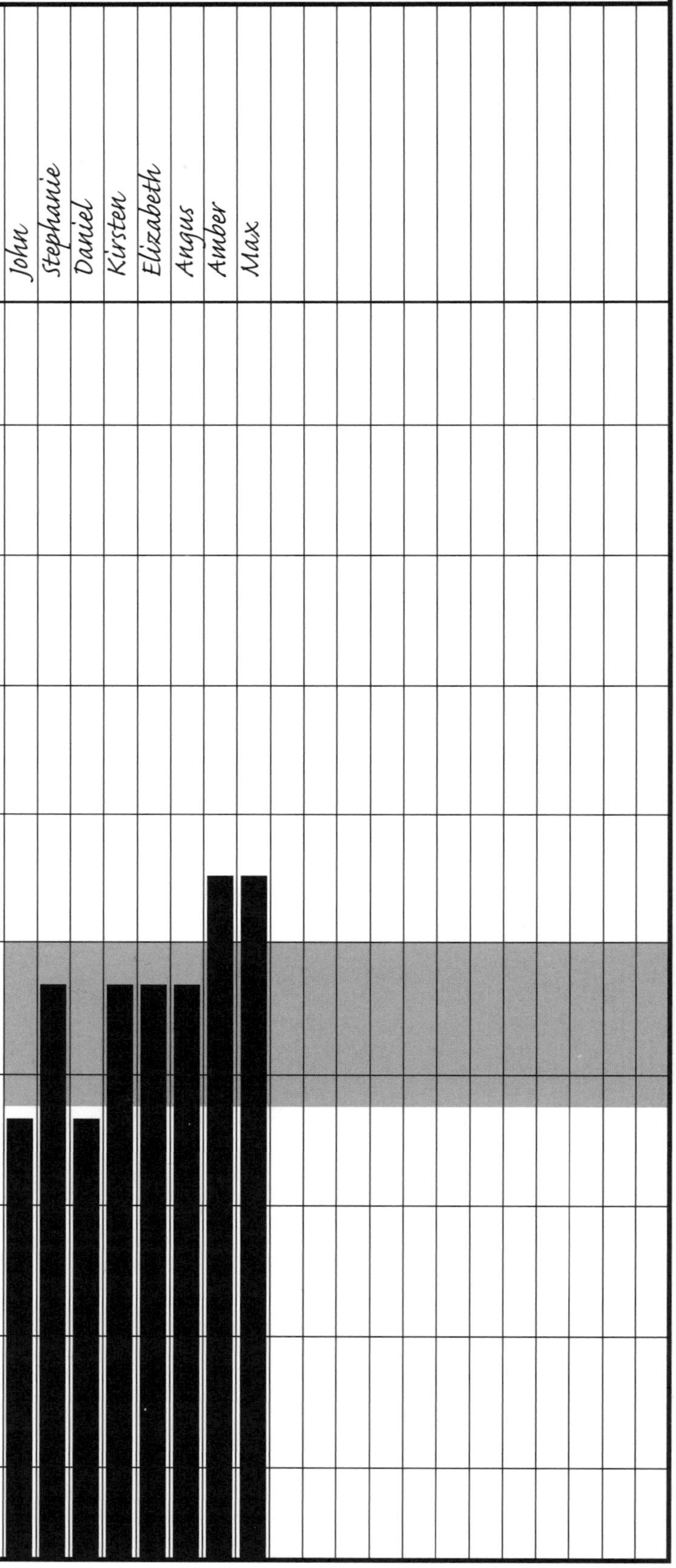

Figure 9.3

Chapter 10

Establishing normative data on teacher judgment

Monitoring learning can occur at a number of levels in an education system, and for several purposes. Within the classroom, we can monitor performance levels of individuals to ensure that they are making progress and that their levels of performance are within the expected standard for their year or age group.

At the building level, it is possible for buildings to obtain evidence regarding overall standards and trends in performance over time. For example, building reporting in terms of profiles to districts, states or national systems can be provided with data from participating schools in a form that enables them to compare their achievement levels with state or district norms.

The ways in which profiles are used for monitoring purposes should be governed by the consequences for those involved. Where the stakes are low, local school building-focused assessment linked to the profiles is likely to be a highly cost-effective means of obtaining comparable information on standards, and it could be the way in which buildings generally respond to the challenge of monitoring standards and evaluating programs.

Where the stakes are high, however, as in system-level monitoring of standards, some will argue that it may be inappropriate to rely entirely upon classroom-based teacher judgments. But this argument also applies to any system that relies on a single approach to assessment in high-stakes exercises. It is just as inappropriate to rely on one test in any area of learning — no matter how many items it contains, the test is a one-time assessment; specially developed tests or assessment tasks that facilitate reporting in terms of the profiles are needed so that a consistent approach is developed. Then there is the so called 'objective' test measure, and the wide-ranging assessment based on continuous observation and professional judgment. The standardized objective test can be used as another form of moderation: this is statistical moderation. Because of the research that has shown that the reliability of teacher judgment grows over time, it is possible to advise systems that monitor educational standards to take the opportunity to modify their survey testing programs and use reporting in terms of the profiles as well as in terms of their own tests. Similar results can be expected — higher and higher reliabilities of teacher judgments.

Teachers from many schools in many states have assisted us in providing ratings for the profiles. The ratings illustrate the students' progress in language arts, using the profiles as a basis. The method of collecting the data was relatively simple, as shown in the instructions that were given to teachers regarding reading-related behavior.

The ratings for a small group from a Sixth Grade class at the start of the school year are shown in the

Read the description of reading-related behavior in the profile bands labelled A through I. Compare each student's behavior pattern with the patterns described at each band level and use the following codes.

3 If the student has established the behavior pattern and consistently exhibits all or most of the behavior in the band, use code 3.

2 If the student is developing behavior patterns such that some but not all of the behavior for a band if often exhibited, use code 2.

1 If the student is beginning to show some of the behavior pattern of a band level in that only a little of the pattern is shown, use code 1.

0 If the student shows none of the behavior patterns for a band level, use a code of 0 for that band.

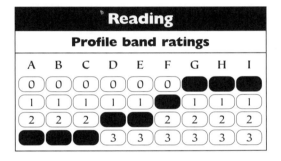

Reading
Profile band ratings

A	B	C	D	E	F	G	H	I
0	0	0	0	0	0	■	■	■
1	1	1	1	1	■	1	1	1
2	2	2	■	■	2	2	2	2
■	■	■	3	3	3	3	3	3

following table. All students were rated 3 (established) in bands A and B and all were rated 0 (no evidence) in band G, so these extremes are not presented.

Rating patterns of students in a small group

	Band C	Band D	Band E	Band F
John	2	1	0	0
Stephanie	3	2	0	0
Daniel	2	2	1	0
Kirsten	3	2	1	0
Elizabeth	3	2	1	0
Angus	3	2	1	0
Amber	3	2	1	1
Max	3	2	2	1

The teacher could quickly place Max, an example of a very keen ten-year-old reader, on the reading scale. Max has been described in all his previous reports as a quietly confident leader in both small and large groups. He has many interests, being a keen sportsman and a talented musician who sings in the choir and plays the piano, the guitar and the saxophone. He has many experiences to bring to his reading. Max writes in his

Writing profile class record

Class ....4.... School ....Brooklyn Elementary School....

Teacher ....Ms Dragila....

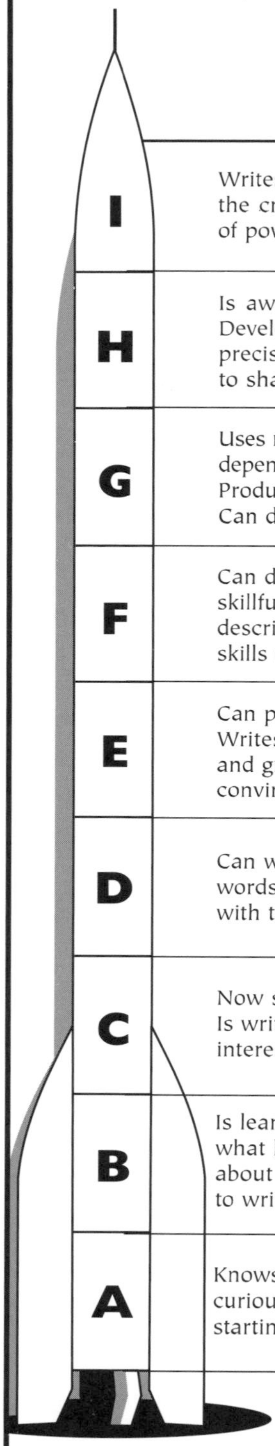

Band		John	Stephanie	Daniel	Kirsten	Elizabeth	Angus	Amber	Max										
I	Writes in many genres. Masters the craft of writing. Is capable of powerful writing.																		
H	Is aware of subtleties in language. Develops analytical arguments. Uses precise descriptions in writing. Edits to sharpen message.																		
G	Uses rich vocabulary, and writing style depends on topic, purpose and audience. Produces lively and colorful writing. Can do major revisions of writing.																		
F	Can describe things well. Can skillfully write and tell a story or describe phenomena. Now has skills to improve writing.																		
E	Can plan, organize and polish writing. Writes in paragraphs. Uses vocabulary and grammar suited to topic. Can write convincing stories.																		
D	Can write own stories. Changes words and spelling until satisfied with the result.																		
C	Now says something in own writing. Is writing own sentences. Is taking interest in appearance of writing.																		
B	Is learning about handwriting. Knows what letters and words are and can talk about ideas in own writing. Is starting to write recognizable letters and words.																		
A	Knows that writing says something. Is curious about environmental print. Is starting to see patterns.																		

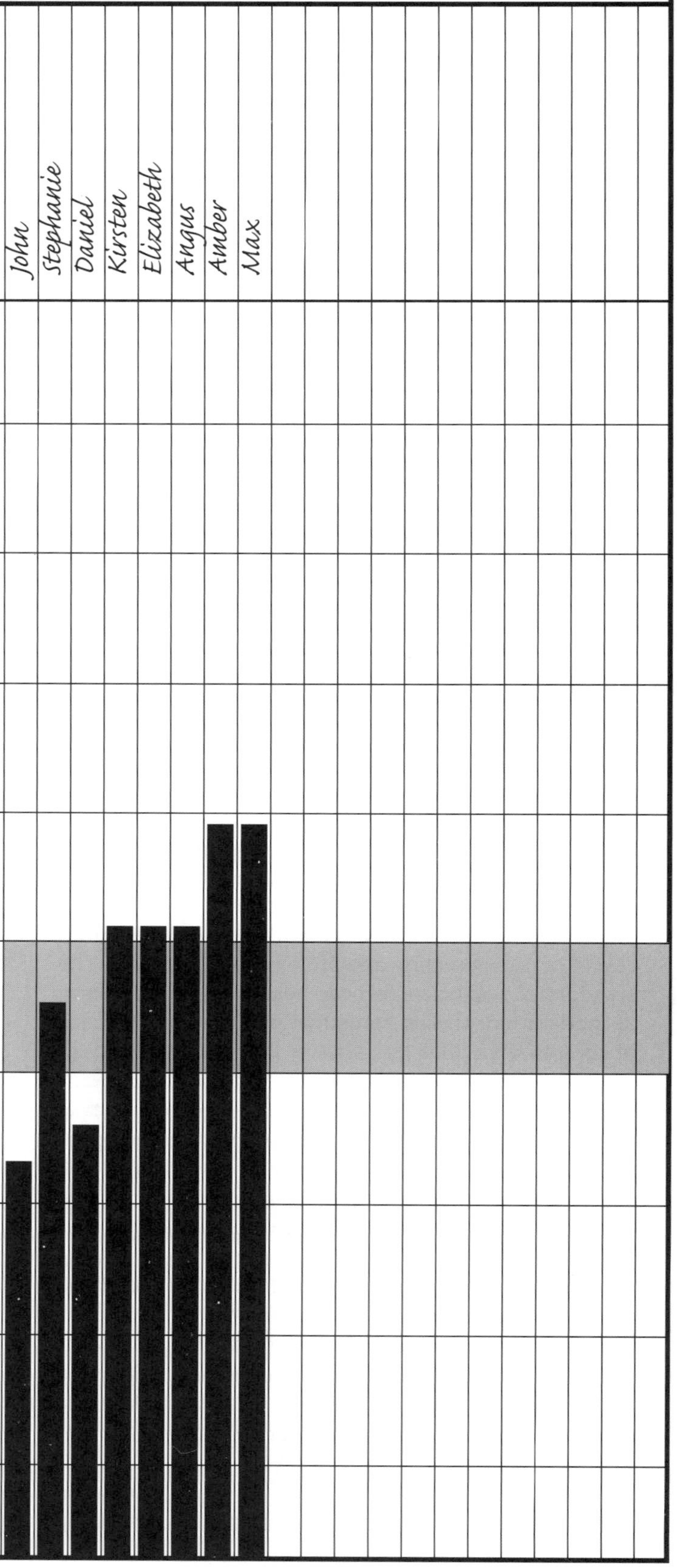

Figure 10.1

self-evaluation that he particularly enjoys writer's workshop times and wants to be a writer like his father. His mother is a keen reader and they often talk about books together. His reading log showed her influence in encouraging him to read classics such as *Treasure Island*, although he makes interesting choices of his own. Max has established all reading behaviors indicated in band C, is developing those in bands D and E and is beginning to use some of the strategies listed in band F. These indicators synthesize much of the information that can be gained intuitively from the above description. Max is shown to be a reader who can talk about what he has read. He absorbs language and ideas. He knows how to tackle a difficult text and read silently for extended periods. Figure 10.1 shows how these ratings are mapped onto the profiles for an overview of a class. Adjustments can be made when teachers judge that progress is evident: the adjustment is simply a matter of adding to the felt-pen mark on the profile. The advantages of passing this class-level information from teacher to teacher are many.

This has further applications when ratings are collected from many schools; a series of box and whisker plots can be used to present the data and to establish norms. A box and whisker plot provides a simple way of presenting normative data and distributions of scores on the profile scales.

Using the rating scale for the profiles in this way enables plots of the data to be produced representing patterns across schools or districts. The box and whisker plots present several pieces of information (see Figure 10.2). For each group, the 10th and 90th percentiles are drawn at the end of the 'whiskers'. The box marks off the 25th and 75th percentiles and the median is marked by a point inside the box. As such, the plots present several distributions simultaneously and allow comparisons across year levels. The star indicates the median score of the distribution.

A series of schools were surveyed and ratings were gathered from teachers over a large range of classes. Box and whisker plots for reading, writing and spoken language scales are presented in Figure 10.3.

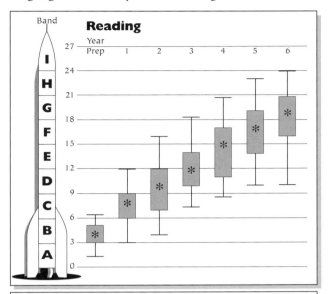

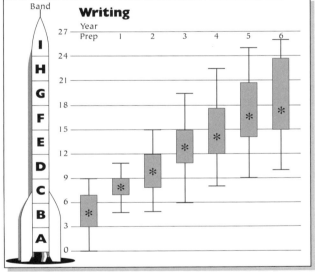

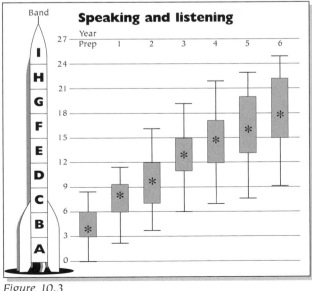

Figure 10.3

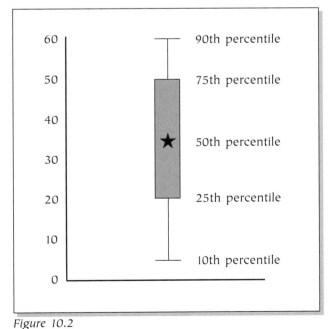

Figure 10.2

Approximately 1000 students were rated in twenty-seven schools across the United States, and larger numbers of students have been surveyed in Ireland and Australia; however, although these should not be considered norms in the true sense of the word, the similarity in the distributions and box plots is striking.

Information of the type represented in Figure 10.3 gives a picture of the progress of *groups of students*. The graphs indicate a period of rapid growth over the first few years of schooling, coinciding with the period during which young people acquire basic literacy skills. Thereafter, a steady and consistent rate of growth is indicated up to Tenth Grade. It is noticeable, however, that the range of achievement increases markedly over the early years of schooling, with more than four levels separating students at the 10th and 90th percentiles. A feature of the graph is the flat growth trajectory for low-achieving students. It shows that achievement levels of students at the 10th percentile increase by less than one band between Fourth and Tenth Grade. These charts have been used to establish the normative regions in the rockets, the class records and the growth charts used in Chapter 8.

Given the cumulative nature of the scales, the established behaviors should reflect this. Students can be developing more than one band-level behavior at any one time; reading development is a continuous process, and the time of the school year needs to be stipulated. If these figures represented the whole system it is evident that by the spring, when most data were collected, the number of students in the system that had fully developed each band level and progressed toward literacy could be stipulated. This would have some implications for curriculum planning and could be treated in much the same way as a cumulative score distribution on a standardized test. Of more interest, however, is the proportion of students who are still developing behaviors or skills at each band level. This can be interpreted as the students' instructional level.

Appendixes

Nutshell statements for profiles

Band	Reading	Writing	Speaking and listening
A	Knows how a book works. Likes to have books and stories read. Likes to talk about stories. Displays reading-like behavior.	Knows that writing says something. Is curious about environmental print. Is starting to see patterns.	Understands social conventions of spoken language and responds appropriately. Listens attentively, interacts with the speaker and responds with interest.
B	Recognizes many familiar words. Attempts new words. Will retell story from a book. Is starting to become an active reader. Is interested in own writing.	Is learning about handwriting. Knows what letters and words are and can talk about ideas in own writing. Is starting to write recognizable letters and words.	Experiments and uses language in a variety of ways. Uses talk to clarify ideas and experiences. Uses body language to assist in conveying understanding. Listens for a range of purposes, discriminates sounds in words, and can recall stories told.
C	Looks for meaning in text. Reading and discussion of text shows enjoyment of reading. Shares experience with others.	Now says something in own writing. Is writing own sentences. Is taking interest in appearance of writing.	Is developing confidence with spoken language. Is sensitive to voice control in specific situations. Is developing confidence through active listening, responding, and clarifying when meaning is not clear.
D	Expects and anticipates sense and meaning in text. Discussion reflects grasp of whole meanings. Now absorbs ideas and language.	Can write own stories. Changes words and spelling until satisfied with the result.	Can recount and retell, recite with feeling, and use a range of vocabulary to arouse and maintain audience interest. Distinguishes between social and informational listening; will seek clarification.
E	Will tackle difficult texts. Writing and general knowledge reflect reading. Literacy response reflects confidence in settings and character.	Can plan, organize and polish writing. Writes in paragraphs. Uses vocabulary and grammar suited to topic. Can write convincing stories.	Uses logic, argument and questioning to clarify ideas and understanding appropriate to audience and purpose. Accepts others' opinions and is developing listening strategies — listening for relationships in stories, poems, etc.

Band	Reading	Writing	Speaking and listening
F	Is familiar with a range of genres. Can interpret, analyze and explain responses to text passages.	Can describe things well. Can skillfully write and tell a story or describe phenomena. Now has skills to improve writing.	Can persuade and influence peers, using language. Clarifies and orders thoughts in conversation. Expresses ideas, feelings, opinions, and can generalize or hypothesize. Can infer meanings when appropriate. Links stories and spoken forms of language to values. Is aware of relevance and irrelevance, pitch intensity, and intonation.
G	Reads for learning as well as pleasure. Reads widely and draws ideas and issues together. Is developing a critical approach to analysis of ideas and writing.	Uses rich vocabulary, and writing style depends on topic, purpose and audience. Produces lively and colorful writing. Can do major revision of writing.	Uses language increasingly to explore ideas, question, and summarize discussions. Uses tone to create effect and to aid communication. Explores and reflects on ideas while listening. Is becoming familiar with a range of spoken forms of language and is able to distinguish between them for purpose, meaning, and appropriate audience.
H	Is clear about own purpose for reading. Reads beyond literal text, and seeks deeper meaning. Can relate social implications to text.	Is aware of subtleties in language. Develops analytical arguments. Uses precise descriptions in writing. Edits to sharpen message.	Uses and appreciates nuances of language to affect an audience. Monitors and modifies communication to aid understanding. Distinguishes emotive rhetoric from reasoned argument. Analyzes spoken genres for meaning and underlying messages.
I	Is skillful in analyzing and interpreting own response to reading. Can respond to a wide range of text styles.	Writes in many genres. Masters the craft of writing. Is capable of powerful writing.	Uses language proficiently in its many forms. Is able to evaluate and respond to content and points of view. Is a skilled listener, able to distinguish emotive and persuasive rhetoric and to analyze a wide range of spoken genres while listening.

Band levels

Band	Reading	Writing	Speaking and listening
A	**Concepts about print** Holds the book right way up. Turns pages from front to back. On request, indicates the beginnings and ends of sentences. Distinguishes between upper and lower case letters. Indicates the start and end of a book.	**What the writer does** Uses writing implement to make marks on paper. Explains the meaning of marks (word, sentence, writing, letter). Copies 'words' from signs in immediate environment. 'Reads', understands and explains own 'writing'.	**Uses of language** Joins in familiar songs, poems and chants. Allows others to speak without unnecessary interruption. Waits for appropriate turn to speak. Offers personal opinion in discussion. Speaks fluently to the class. Follows instructions, directions and explanations. Listens attentively to stories, songs and poems. Reacts to stories, songs and poems heard in class (smiles and comments). Recognises sounds in the environment. Begins to recall details. Begins to sequence. Follows directions during classroom routines.
	Reading strategies Locates words, lines, spaces, letters. Refers to letters by name. Locates own name and other familiar words in a short text. Identifies known, familiar words in other contexts.	**What the writing shows** Understanding of the difference between picture and print. Use of some recognizable symbols found in writing.	**Features of language** Connects phrases and clauses with 'and', 'and then', 'but'. Speaks at a rate that enables others to follow. Speaks at a volume appropriate to the situation. Hears sounds and does actions simultaneously in action songs. Hears rhyming words.
	Responses Responds to literature (smiles, claps, listens intently). Joins in familiar stories.	**Use of writing** Comments on signs and other symbols in immediate environment. Uses a mixture of drawings and 'writing' to convey and support an idea.	
	Interests and attitudes Shows preference for particular books. Chooses books as a free-time activity.		
B	**Reading strategies** Takes risks when reading. 'Reads' books with simple, repetitive language patterns. 'Reads', understands and explains own 'writing'. Is aware that print tells a story. Uses pictures for clues to meaning of text. Asks others for help with meaning and pronunciation of words. Consistently reads familiar words and interprets symbols within a text. Predicts words. Matches known clusters of letters to clusters in unknown words. Locates own name and other familiar words in a short text. Uses knowledge of words in the environment when 'reading' and 'writing'. Uses various strategies to follow a line of print. Copies classroom print, labels, signs, etc.	**What the writer does** Reproduces words from signs and other sources in immediate environment. Holds pencil/pen using satisfactory grip. Uses preferred hand consistently for writing. Attempts to put 'words' in 'sentence' format. 'Writes' a simple message. Uses sound–symbol linkages. 'Captions' or 'labels' drawings.	**Uses of language** Makes short announcements clearly. Tells personal anecdotes in discussion. Retells a story heard in class, preserving the sequence of events. Accurately conveys a verbal message to another person. Responds with facial expressions. Responds with talk when others initiate conversation. Initiates conversation with peers. Holds conversation with familiar adults. Asks what unfamiliar words mean. Uses talk to clarify ideas or experience. Listens and sustains attention for increasing periods. Talks about mental pictures after listening to stories, poems etc. Identifies meaning from speaker's voice (anger, surprise). Selects and gives options in listening activities.
	Responses Selects own books to 'read'. Describes connections among events in texts. Writes, role-plays and/or draws in response to a story or other form of writing (e.g. poem, message). Creates ending when text is left unfinished. Recounts parts of text in writing, drama or artwork. Retells, using language expressions from reading sources. Retells with approximate sequence.	**What the writing shows** Use of vocabulary of print (letters, words, question marks, etc.). Use of letters of the alphabet and other conventional symbols. Use of letters in groups to form words. Placing of spaces between groups of 'letters'. Knowledge that writing moves from left to right in lines from top to bottom of page.	**Features of language** Reacts to absurd word-substitution. Demonstrates an appreciation of wit. Reacts to unusual features of language such as rhythm, alliteration or onomatopoeia. Hears initial and final sounds in words.
	Interests and attitudes Explores a variety of books. Begins to show an interest in specific type of literature. Plays at reading books. Talks about favorite books.	**Use of writing** Writes own name. **Interests and attitudes** Understands that writing is talk written down.	

Band	Reading	Writing	Speaking and listening

C

Reading strategies

Rereads a paragraph or sentence to establish meaning. Uses context as a basis for predicting meaning of unfamiliar words. Reads aloud, showing understanding of purpose of punctuation marks. Uses picture cues to make appropriate responses for unknown words. Uses pictures to help read a text. Finds where another reader is up to in a reading passage.

Responses

Writing and artwork reflect understanding of text. Retells, discusses and expresses opinions on literature, and reads further. Recalls events and characters spontaneously from text.

Interests and attitudes

Seeks recommendations for books to read. Chooses more than one type of book. Chooses to read when given free choice. Concentrates on reading for lengthy periods.

What the writer does

Commences writing without assistance. Has a personalized handwriting style that meets most handwriting needs. Checks written work by reading it aloud. Sounds out words as an aid to spelling.

What the writing shows

Legible writing with recognizable words. Words put together in sentence format. Words written in a logical order to make a sentence that can be read. Upper and lower case letters used conventionally. Written sentences that can be understood by an adult.

Use of writing

Sentences convey message on one topic. Uses 'I' in writing. Writes about feelings, judgment or direct experience. Creates characters from experience and immediate environment.

Uses of language

Makes verbal commentary during play or other activities with concrete objects. Speaks confidently in formal situations (assembly, report to class). Explains ideas clearly in discussion. Discusses information heard (e.g. dialogue, news items, report). Based on consideration of what has already been said, offers personal opinions. Asks for repetition, restatement or general explanation to clarify meaning. Is aware of non-verbal communication. Is learning to listen critically for main idea and supporting details. Awareness of the need to be silent, to wait and respond as appropriate. Ability to distinguish between types of speech (a chat, a warning, a joke). Listens to plan, compare and begin to make judgments.

Features of language

Sequences a presentation in logical order. Gives instructions in a concise and understandable manner. Reads aloud with expression, showing awareness of rhythm and tone. Modulates voice for effect. Nods, looks at speaker when others initiate talk. Hears middle sounds in words.

D

Reading strategies

Reads material with a wide variety of styles and topics. Selects books to fulfill own purposes. States main idea in a passage. Substitutes words with similar meanings when reading aloud. Self-corrects, using knowledge of language structure and sound–symbol relationships. Predicts, using knowledge of language structure and/or sound/symbol to make sense of a word or a phrase.

Responses

Discusses different types of reading materials. Discusses materials read at home. Tells a variety of audiences about a book. Uses vocabulary and sentence structure from reading materials in written work as well as in conversation. Uses themes from reading in artwork. Follows written instructions.

Interests and attitudes

Recommends books to others. Reads often. Reads silently for extended periods.

What the writer does

Marks most common words with incorrect spelling when editing writing. Uses ideas, themes and structure from books in writing. Uses concepts of order and time in writing. Reads, rereads and revises own written work. Uses everyday words in appropriate written context.

What the writing shows

Punctuation used conventionally. Conventional spelling used most of the time; spelling showing recall of visual patterns. Stories that can be read, understood and retold by classmates. Several sentences constructed on one topic in a logical order. A smooth connection of ideas. Beginning, middle and end in narrative writing.

Use of writing

Writes stories containing characters from outside personal environment. Writes with ease on most matters of personal experience. Writes on a variety of topics. Writes personal anecdotes and letters to friends. Writes for a known audience. Uses a range of written forms — poems, letters, journals, logs, etc.

Uses of language

Tells personal anecdotes, illustrating in a relevant way the issue being discussed. Recounts a story or repeats a song spontaneously. Retells scenes from a film or drama. Offers predictions about what will come next. Recites poems. Asks questions in conversation. Has a second try at something to make it more precise. Arouses and maintains an audience interest during formal presentations (e.g. report to class, announcement). Hears the difference between social interactions and information transaction.

Features of language

Uses a range of vocabulary related to a particular topic. Maintains receptive body stance in conversation. Speaks in a way that conveys feelings (while keeping emotions under control). Hears consonants, vowels, blends and digraphs. Hears the difference between hard and soft vowels. Ability to listen to and recognise and give an explanation (e.g. in science). Asks for repetition or an explanation when meaning is unclear. Is able to listen to make judgments, summarize and evaluate.

Band	Reading	Writing	Speaking and listening

E

Reading strategies

Reads to others with few inappropriate pauses. Interprets new words by reference to suffixes, prefixes and meaning of word parts. Uses directories such as a table of contents or an index, or telephone and street directories, to locate information. Uses library classification systems to find specific reading materials.

Responses

Improvises in role play, drawing on a range of text. Writing shows meaning inferred from the text. Explains a piece of literature. Expresses and supports an opinion on whether an author's point of view is valid. Discusses implied motives of characters in the text. Makes comments and expresses feelings about characters. Rewrites information from text in own words. Uses text as a model for own writing. Uses a range of books and print materials as information sources for written work. Reads aloud with appropriate expression.

What the writer does

Edits work to a point where others can read it; corrects common spelling errors, punctuation and grammatical errors. Develops ideas into paragraphs. Uses a dictionary, thesaurus or word-checker to extend and check vocabulary for writing. Uses vivid, specific language.

What the writing shows

Sentences with ideas that flow. Paragraphs with a cohesive structure. Ability to present relationships and to argue or persuade. Messages in expository and argumentative writing identifiable by others, although some information may be omitted. Brief passages written with clear meaning, accuracy of spelling and apt punctuation. Appropriate shifts from first to third person in writing. Consistent use of the correct tense. Appropriate vocabulary for familiar audiences such as peers, younger children or adults, with only occasional inappropriate word choice. Compound sentences, using conjunctions. Variations of letters, print styles or fonts. A print style appropriate to task and a consistent handwriting style.

Use of writing

Writes a properly sequenced text with a convincing setting. Creates characters from imagination.

Uses of language

Presents a point of view to a large audience. Presents materials with consideration for audience needs. Speculates and puts forward a tentative proposition. Uses logic, arguments or appeals to feelings to persuade others. Explores concepts related to concrete materials by describing, narrating or explaining how things work and why things happen. Dramatizes familiar stories, showing understanding. Uses convincing dialogue to role-play short scenes involving familiar situations or emotions. Invites others to participate. Takes initiative in raising new aspects of an issue. Asks questions to elicit more from an individual. Answers questions confidently and clearly in interviews. Asks for the meaning of familiar words used in unfamiliar ways. Listens to compare and find relationships in stories, poems, and conversations. Listens to analyze and hypothesize.

Features of language

Makes links between ideas in discussions. Uses complex connectives in speech, such as 'although', 'in spite of', 'so that'. Uses syntactical structures — principal and subordinate clauses. Uses vocabulary appropriate to audience and purpose. Distinguishes between words of similar meaning. Identifies the sounds of vowels, consonants, digraphs and blends. Uses awareness of sounds to identify consonants and vowels. Uses sounds to identify prefixes, suffixes, compounds and syllables.

F

Reading strategies

Describes links between personal experience and arguments and ideas in text. Selects relevant passages or phrases to answer questions without necessarily reading whole text. Formulates research topics and questions and finds relevant information from reading materials. Maps out plots and character developments in novels and other literary texts. Varies reading strategies according to purposes for reading and nature of text. Makes connections between texts, recognising similarities of themes and values.

Responses

Discusses author's intent for the reader. Discusses styles used by different authors. Describes settings in literature. Forms generalizations about a range of genres, including myth, short story. Offers reasons for the feelings provoked by a text. Writing and discussions acknowledge a range of interpretations of text. Offers critical opinion or analysis of reading passages in discussion. Justifies own appraisal of a text. Synthesizes and expands on information from a range of texts in written work.

What the writer does

Writes sentences in different forms: statement, question, command, explanation. Writes paragraphs to develop logical sequence of ideas. Corrects most spelling, punctuation and grammatical errors in editing others' written work. Consults available sources to improve or enhance writing. Joins letters, using linkages where appropriate, to form personal handwriting style.

What the writing shows

Narratives containing introduction, complication and resolution in a logical order. Longer descriptions and narratives developed coherently. Use of both active and passive voice. A range of vocabulary and grammatical structures. Complex sentences — principal and subordinate clauses. Higher level writing skills in areas of special interest. Understanding of the difference between narrative and other forms of writing.

Use of writing

Completes standard forms requiring personal information. Makes appropriate use of narrative and other forms of writing.

Uses of language

Asks speaker to clarify ambiguities. Asks questions to draw information from the group. Indicates disagreement in a constructive manner. Attempts to resolve disagreement or misunderstanding. Supports constructively the statements of others. Attempts to keep discussion on the topic. Makes formal introductions with courtesy and clarity. Tells a story with expression and emphasis, showing confidence, highlighting key points and demonstrating the storyteller's art. Explores abstract ideas (justice, good and evil) by generalizing, hypothesizing or inferring. Uses thinking skills in listening activities to hypothesize.

Features of language

Uses a range of idiomatic expressions with confidence. Reacts to an inappropriate choice of words. Makes positive interjections. Distinguishes intensity, pitch, quality and sequence of a variety of sounds.

Band	Reading	Writing	Speaking and listening

G

Reading strategies

Reads manuals and literature of varying complexity. Interprets simple maps, tables and graphs in the context of discursive text. Makes generalizations and draws conclusions from reading. Reads at different speeds, using scanning, skim-reading or careful reading as appropriate.

Responses

Supports argument or opinion by reference to evidence presented in sources outside text. Compares information from different sources. Identifies opposing points of view and main and supporting arguments in text. Comments on cohesiveness of text as a whole. Discusses and writes about author's bias and technique. In writing, offers critical opinion or analysis of reading materials. Distils and links ideas from complex sentences and paragraphs.

Interests and attitudes

Reads widely for pleasure, for interest or for learning.

What the writer does

Writes in narrative, expository and argumentative styles. Uses a range of writing styles effectively and appropriately for purpose, situation and audience. Uses a range of vocabulary effectively and appropriately for purpose, situation and audience. Edits work to improve the smooth flow of ideas and reorganizes work to make it more readable. Replaces words and sentences during revision of written work. Changes sequence of ideas, adds new ideas during revision.

What the writing shows

Main and supporting ideas presented clearly. Correct format for letters, invitations. Figurative language, such as simile, for descriptive purposes.

Use of writing

Shows a range of styles — written conversations, poems, plays, journals. Writes formal and social letters and distinguishes between the purposes of each. Adapts writing to demands of task. Completes complex forms that seek detailed biographical and related information.

Uses of language

Asks interview questions that are relevant. Extends another group member's contribution by elaboration or illustration. Helps others to put forward ideas. Summarizes the conclusions reached in a group discussion. Takes initiative in moving discussion to the next stage. Reflects and evaluates discussion (e.g. What have we learned? How did we do it?). Dramatizes scenes from complex stories, showing understanding of dramatic structure. Uses appropriate introductions and conclusions according to purpose and context. Identifies and uses different strategies for responding to listener feedback. Responds to audience by adjusting features such as pace, tone or volume, to sustain interest.

Features of language

Varies tone, pitch, pace of speech to create effect and aid communication. Self-corrects a poor choice of words. Talks or writes about special forms of language, such as accents or dialects. Identifies and discusses the typical structures and features of poems, songs, fables, advertisements, speeches and commentaries.

H

Reading strategies

Compiles own list of needed references, using bibliographies and literature-search techniques. Interprets material at different levels of meaning. Forms generalizations about a range of genres, including myth, short story. Lists a wide variety of sources read for specific learning tasks.

Responses

Identifies plot and subplot. Identifies allegory. Formulates hypothetical questions about a subject, based on prior reading. Compares and offers critical analysis of materials presented in the media. Extracts ideas embedded in complex passages of text. Displays critical opinion and analysis in written reports of reading. Identifies different authors' points of view on a topic. Reformulates a task in the light of available reading resources. Questions and reflects on issues encountered in texts. Shows understanding by being able to adopt an alternative point of view to the author's. Discusses styles used by different authors.

What the writer does

Edits and revises own work to enhance effect of vocabulary, text organization and layout. Edits and revises others' writing, improving presentation and structure without losing meaning or message.

What the writing shows

Meaning expressed precisely. Organization and layout of written text accurate and appropriate for purpose, situation and audience. Argument, description and narrative presented effectively and appropriately. Vocabulary showing awareness of ambiguities and shades of meaning. Figurative language, such as metaphor, to convey meaning.

Use of writing

Presents analysis of argument and situation. Sustains organization of ideas, which are justified with detail in extended writing.

Uses of language

Experiments with and reflects on possible readings and interpretations of a piece of scripted drama. Sustains cogent arguments in formal presentation. Holds conversation with less familiar adults (e.g. guest speaker). Contributes to group discussions, Is able to give considered reasons for own opinions. Gives prepared talks presenting some challenging themes and issues. Is able to use technology such as an overhead projector or data-show projector to enhance communication. Is able to find implied or stated meanings after listening to persuasive speeches. Listens to spoken texts with challenging themes and issues and is able to summarize the main issues.

Features of language

Defines or explains words to cater for audience needs. Comments on bias or point of view in spoken language. Analyzes factors that contribute to the success or otherwise of discussion. Identifies how linguistic features, such as emotive language, humour and anecdotes, can be used to engage audiences.

Band	Reading	Writing	Speaking and listening

I

Reading strategies
Examines situational meaning of text. Explores a range of meaning dependent on the combination of influences of writer, reader and situation.

Responses
Explains textual innuendo and undertone. Interprets analogy, allegory and parable in text. Identifies and explains deeper significance in text. Defends each interpretation of text. Discusses and writes about author's bias. Analyzes cohesiveness of text as a whole.

What the writer does
Writes with ease on most familiar topics in both short passages and extended writing. Uses analogies and symbolism in writing. Uses irony in writing. Uses figures of speech, metaphor and simile to illustrate and support message embedded in extended text. Structures a convincing argument in writing. Can use sustained and elaborated metaphorical language in writing.

What the writing shows
Extension beyond conventions of standard written English in a skillful and effective way.

Use of writing
Conveys extended arguments through writing. Adapts to demands of academic writing.

Uses of language
Makes effective use of visual or other materials to illustrate ideas. Capitalizes on opportunities offered by responses to interview questions. Asks interview questions designed to elicit extended responses. Participates effectively in debates, meetings and other structured situations characterised by complexity of purpose, procedure and subject matter. Combines improvised and prepared text to engage and entertain audience. Listens to a range of spoken texts, such as radio or television interviews, before taking part in critical discussion. Thinks about sociocultural background, age and knowledge of speaker in panel or interviews in order to frame appropriate questions.

Features of language
Talks or writes about subtle effects of dialogue between characters in film or drama. Uses puns and double meanings. Comments on tone, attitude or emphasis in speech. Talks about quality of speech, such as loudness, pitch, pronunciation, articulation and dialect. Stresses key words to ensure audience attentiveness and understanding. Uses pauses to emphasize important points. Selects aspects of written research assignment for presentation in speech, making necessary adjustments to style and content. Controls pitch, timing, sequencing of content and style of delivery to maximize the impact of spoken texts presenting complex themes or issues. Listens to and builds on the ideas of others. Listens to and challenges the ideas of others through questions, asking for clarification. Evaluates elements of persuasion and appeal in spoken texts. Is able to identify the subtle ways in which spoken language can be used to manipulate an audience. Is able to adopt appropriate language conventions in formal speech settings.

Appendix III

Blackline masters

Reading profile rocket

Class .... School ....

Teacher .... Student ....

I — Is skillful in analyzing and interpreting own response to reading. Can respond to a wide range of text styles.

Is clear about own purpose for reading. Reads beyond literal text, and seeks deeper meaning. Can relate social implications to text. — **H**

G — Reads for learning as well as pleasure. Reads widely and draws ideas and issues together. Is developing a critical approach to analysis of ideas and writing.

Is familiar with a range of genres. Can interpret, analyze and explain responses to text passages. — **F**

E — Will tackle difficult texts. Writing and general knowledge reflect reading. Literacy response reflects confidence in settings and character.

Expects and anticipates sense and meaning in text. Discussion reflects grasp of whole meanings. Now absorbs ideas and language. — **D**

C — Looks for meaning in text. Reading and discussion of text shows enjoyment of reading. Shares experience with others.

Recognizes many familiar words. Attempts new words. Will retell story from a book. Is starting to become an active reader. Is interested in own writing. — **B**

A — Knows how a book works. Likes to have books and stories read. Likes to talk about stories. Displays reading-like behavior.

50% of the ☐ Grade students can be located within this range. Norms for all grades can be identified by locating the 'box' from the box and whisker plot in Chapter 10 for the relevant skill.

The student is estimated to be at about this location on the profile. See the worked example from writing shown on pages 98–100.

Writing profile rocket

Class .... School ....

Teacher .... Student ....

I — — — — — Writes in many genres. Masters the craft of writing. Is capable of powerful writing.

Is aware of subtleties in language. Develops analytical arguments. Uses precise descriptions in writing. Edits to sharpen message. — — — — — **H**

G — — — — — Uses rich vocabulary, and writing style depends on topic, purpose and audience. Produces lively and colorful writing. Can do major revision of writing.

Can describe things well. Can skillfully write and tell a story or describe phenomena. Now has skills to improve writing. — — — — — **F**

E — — — — — Can plan, organize and polish writing. Writes in paragraphs. Uses vocabulary and grammar suited to topic. Can write convincing stories.

Can write own stories. Changes words and spelling until satisfied with the result. — — — — — **D**

C — — — — — Now says something in own writing. Is writing own sentences. Is taking interest in appearance of writing.

Is learning about handwriting. Knows what letters and words are and can talk about ideas in own writing. Is starting to write recognizable letters and words. — — — — — **B**

A — — — — — Knows that writing says something. Is curious about environmental print. Is starting to see patterns.

▨ 50% of the ☐ Grade students can be located within this range. Norms for all grades can be identified by locating the 'box' from the box and whisker plot in Chapter 10 for the relevant skill.

■ The student is estimated to be at about this location on the profile. See the worked example from writing shown on pages 98–100.

Speaking and listening profile rocket

Class .... School ....

Teacher .... Student ....

Uses and appreciates nuances of language to affect an audience. Monitors and modifies communication to aid understanding. Distinguishes emotive rhetoric from reasoned argument. Analyzes spoken genres for meaning and underlying messages.

Can persuade and influence peers, using language. Clarifies and orders thoughts in conversation. Expresses ideas, feelings, opinions, and can generalize or hypothesize. Can infer meanings when appropriate. Links stories and spoken forms of language to values. Is aware of relevance and irrelevance, pitch intensity, and intonation.

Can recount and retell, recite with feeling, and use a range of vocabulary to arouse and maintain audience interest. Distinguishes between social and informational listening; will seek clarification.

Experiments and uses language in a variety of ways. Uses talk to clarify ideas and experiences. Uses body language to assist in conveying understanding. Listens for a range of purposes, discriminates sounds in words, and can recall stories told.

Uses language proficiently in its many forms. Is able to evaluate and respond to content and points of view. Is a skilled listener, able to distinguish emotive and persuasive rhetoric and to analyze a wide range of spoken genres while listening.

Uses language increasingly to explore ideas, question, and summarize discussions. Uses tone to create effect and to aid communication. Explores and reflects on ideas while listening. Is becoming familiar with a range of spoken forms of language and is able to distinguish between them for purpose, meaning, and appropriate audience.

Uses logic, argument and questioning to clarify ideas and understanding appropriate to audience and purpose. Accepts others' opinions and is developing listening strategies — listening for relationships in stories, poems, etc.

Is developing confidence with spoken language. Is sensitive to voice control in specific situations. Is developing confidence through active listening, responding, and clarifying when meaning is not clear.

Understands social conventions of spoken language and responds appropriately. Listens attentively, interacts with the speaker and responds with interest.

I H G F E D C B A

50% of the [ ] Grade students can be located within this range. Norms for all grades can be identified by locating the 'box' from the box and whisker plot in Chapter 10 for the relevant skill.

The student is estimated to be at about this location on the profile. See the worked example from writing shown on pages 98-100.

Reading profile class record

Class ....School ....

Teacher ....

Band

I	Is skillful in analyzing and interpreting own response to reading. Can respond to a wide range of text styles.	
H	Is clear about own purpose for reading. Reads beyond literal text, and seeks deeper meaning. Can relate social implications to text.	
G	Reads for learning as well as pleasure. Reads widely and draws ideas and issues together. Is developing a critical approach to analysis of ideas and writing.	
F	Is familiar with a range of genres. Can interpret, analyze and explain responses to text passages.	
E	Will tackle difficult texts. Writing and general knowledge reflect reading. Literacy response reflects confidence in settings and character.	
D	Expects and anticipates sense and meaning in text. Discussion reflects grasp of whole meanings. Now absorbs ideas and language.	
C	Looks for meaning in text. Reading and discussion of text shows enjoyment of reading. Shares experience with others.	
B	Recognizes many familiar words. Attempts new words. Will retell story from a book. Is starting to become an active reader. Is interested in own writing.	
A	Knows how a book works. Likes to have books and stories read. Likes to talk about stories. Displays reading-like behavior.	

Writing profile class record

Class .... School ....

Teacher ....

Band

I	Writes in many genres. Masters the craft of writing. Is capable of powerful writing.
H	Is aware of subtleties in language. Develops analytical arguments. Uses precise descriptions in writing. Edits to sharpen message.
G	Uses rich vocabulary, and writing style depends on topic, purpose and audience. Produces lively and colorful writing. Can do major revision of writing.
F	Can describe things well. Can skillfully write and tell a story or describe phenomena. Now has skills to improve writing.
E	Can plan, organize and polish writing. Writes in paragraphs. Uses vocabulary and grammar suited to topic. Can write convincing stories.
D	Can write own stories. Changes words and spelling until satisfied with the result.
C	Now says something in own writing. Is writing own sentences. Is taking interest in appearance of writing.
B	Is learning about handwriting. Knows what letters and words are and can talk about ideas in own writing. Is starting to write recognizable letters and words.
A	Knows that writing says something. Is curious about environmental print. Is starting to see patterns.

Speaking and listening profile class record

Class ....School ....

Teacher ....

Band

I	Uses language proficiently in its many forms. Is able to evaluate and respond to content and points of view. Is a skilled listener, able to distinguish emotive and persuasive rhetoric and to analyze a wide range of spoken genres while listening.	
H	Uses and appreciates nuances of language to affect an audience. Monitors and modifies communication to aid understanding. Distinguishes emotive rhetoric from reasoned argument. Analyzes spoken genres for meaning and underlying messages.	
G	Uses language increasingly to explore ideas, question, and summarize discussions. Uses tone to create effect and to aid communication. Explores and reflects on ideas while listening. Is becoming familiar with a range of spoken forms of language and is able to distinguish between them for purpose, meaning, and appropriate audience.	
F	Can persuade and influence peers, using language. Clarifies and orders thoughts in conversation. Expresses ideas, feelings, opinions, and can generalize or hypothesize. Can infer meanings when appropriate. Links stories and spoken forms of language to values. Is aware of relevance and irrelevance, pitch intensity, and intonation.	
E	Uses logic, argument and questioning to clarify ideas and understanding appropriate to audience and purpose. Accepts others' opinions and is developing listening strategies — listening for relationships in stories, poems, etc.	
D	Can recount and retell, recite with feeling, and use a range of vocabulary to arouse and maintain audience interest. Distinguishes between social and informational listening; will seek clarification.	
C	Is developing confidence with spoken language. Is sensitive to voice control in specific situations. Is developing confidence through active listening, responding, and clarifying when meaning is not clear.	
B	Experiments and uses language in a variety of ways. Uses talk to clarify ideas and experiences. Uses body language to assist in conveying understanding. Listens for a range of purposes, discriminates sounds in words, and can recall stories told.	
A	Understands social conventions of spoken language and responds appropriately. Listens attentively, interacts with the speaker and responds with interest.	

Bibliography

Dancing with the Pen: The Learner as a Writer 1996, Ministry of Education (Learning Media), Wellington, New Zealand.

Clay, M.M. 1985, *The Early Detection of Reading Difficulties: A Diagnostic Survey with Recovery Procedures*, Heinemann, Auckland, NZ, 3rd edn.

Dorn, L.J., French, C. & Jones, T. 1998, *Apprenticeship in Literacy*, Stenhouse Publishers, York, Maine.

ECLAS: Early Childhood Literacy Assessment System 1999, New York City Board of Education, New York, NY.

Education Department of Western Australia 1994, *First Steps*, Heinemann, Portsmouth, New Hampshire.

English Language Arts Resource Guide 1998, The State Education Department, Albany, NY.

English Profiles 1991, School Programs Division, Ministry of Education and Training, Melbourne, Victoria, Australia.

Fountas, I. & Pinnell, G. 1996, *Guided Reading: Good First Teaching for All Children*, Heinemann, Portsmouth, New Hampshire.

Graves, D.H. 1983, *Writing: Teachers and Children at Work*, Heinemann, Exeter, New Hampshire.

—— 1994, *A Fresh Look at Writing*, Heinemann, Portsmouth, New Hampshire.

Holdaway, D. 1979, *Foundations of Literacy*, Ashton Scholastic, Sydney, Australia.

Performance Standards, Volume 1: Elementary School, New Standards 1977, National Center on Education and the Economy, University of Pittsburgh, Pennsylvania.

Reading for Life: The Learner as a Reader 1996, Ministry of Education (Learning Media), Wellington, New Zealand.

Rowe, K.J. 1997, *Factors Affecting Student' Progress in Reading: Key Findings from a Longitudinal Study in Research in Reading Recovery*, Heinemann, Portsmouth, New Hampshire.

Snowball, D. & Bolton, F. 1999, *Spelling K–8: Planning and Teaching*, Stenhouse Publishers, York, Maine.

Sunshine Assessment Resource Kit: Grades K–1, 2–3, The Wright Group, Bothell, WA.

Walmsley, S. 1998, *Meeting the Challenge of the New 4th, 8th and 11th Grade: New York State Literacy Assessments*, Department of Reading, University of Albany, NY.